Recently, more Protestants and evangelicals are expressing a renewed interest in the idea of living by a rule of life. Paul Gutacker's book gives greater depth and shape to these conversations, first by showing how the Anglican tradition embodies and commends a rule of life, but also by showing how deeply anchored this practice is in Scripture and in Christian history. I recommend this book to anyone interested in how to follow Christ more intentionally in their time, habits, rhythms, and daily life.

TISH HARRISON WARREN
Author of *Liturgy of the Ordinary* and *Prayer in the Night*

I have seen firsthand the wise and wonderful things Paul Gutacker and his wife, Paige, have done to build vibrant, thoughtful, worshipful community here on the banks of the Brazos. In *Practicing Life Together* Paul has harvested the fruit of his experience and is sharing it with the people of Jesus. For anyone who wants to take Christian community seriously, I can't think of a better guide than this one.

ALAN JACOBS
Distinguished Professor of Humanities in the Honors Program at Baylor University and author of *How to Think*

Brimful of wisdom, this marvelous book calls us to a way of life characterized by love and a serious pursuit of Christ. Drawing deeply on the time-tested traditions of the church, it shows us how to say YES to good and NO to all that hold us back from the true countercultural freedom we long for. Discipline and community are reframed on the pages of this book as a beautiful invitation.

SARAH C. WILLIAMS
Research professor at Regent College, research associate at St Benet's Hall, Oxford, and author of author of *When Courage Calls*

Paul Gutacker's *Practicing Life Together* is a treasure trove

and guidance for community life among Christians. I highly recommend this book to pastors, small group leaders, and any Christians who desire the steady and substantial relationships that the Bible portrays as normative in the church.

THOMAS S. KIDD
Yeats Chair of Baptist Studies, Midwestern Baptist Theological Seminary

There are many decent proposals out there advocating for a "rule of life"—and for good reason: we desperately need them, especially in our anxious, unruled, and rootless age. But Paul Gutacker offers us here something even better: a ruled life in the context of thick spiritual community and deep theological formation. A rule of life, as Gutacker frames it, is no self-help program for solo artists but a sturdy structure founded on the pillars of common prayer, table fellowship, theological study, and vocational discernment. What is more: it really works. This book is written both from careful attention to the Christian tradition and from years of experience working with young adults who have seen real and enduring spiritual growth.

ALEX FOGLEMAN
Associate Dean of Special Programs and Assistant Professor of Theology at Trinity Anglican Seminary, and author of *Knowledge, Faith, and Early Christian Initiation*

This is a book that Paul Gutacker is uniquely qualified to write as a thoughtful leader with years of experience guiding others in their spiritual formation in the sort of church-based, rule-of-life community that is genuinely transformative. We need Christian communities with a culture thick enough, and practices robust enough, to allow faith to establish deep roots. Practical and approachable, this book is filled with the wisdom of the centuries. There is so much hope in the program Paul sets out so clearly here, and my prayer is that this book might stimulate a broad-based movement of spiritual renewal in our churches. Read this book slowly and prayerfully, and then consider planting this sort of community where you live and worship. It will make all the difference.

BRUCE HINDMARSH
James M. Houston Professor of Spiritual Theology and Professor of the History of Christianity, Regent College, Vancouver

All of us are meant to live like monks—committed, together, to a common rule. For nearly a decade now, Paul and Paige Gutacker have invited others to join them in their commitment to eating, praying, studying, and attending together. Drawing on the wisdom of Scripture and tradition, *Practicing Life Together* offers spiritual guidance to redirect our disordered desires toward the freedom found only in Christ. Paul Gutacker doesn't just help us figure out what the good life is, but he offers practices that themselves *are* the good life. Read this book and be inspired by his passion for people, his love of language, and his joy in the journey.

FR. HANS BOERSMA
Saint Benedict Servants of Christ Chair in Ascetical Theology, Nashotah House Theological Seminary

If even 5 percent of small groups in American churches began practicing what Paul Gutacker commends in this book, the church would be radically transformed. We need to meet God in deep, stable, and serious ways—together. This book offers wise counsel and lively encouragement for how to begin. Buy, read, and—most importantly—embrace these practices and discover the life God has for His people.

MATTHEW LEE ANDERSON
Assistant Professor in the Honors Program at Baylor University and author of *Called into Questions*

If you are someone who feels intimidated by a Common Rule of Life, I challenge you to read this book. Rooted in rich history, but situated in the mayhem of modern life, *Practicing Life Together* offers a practical way to engage in the ancient but eternally relevant rhythms of our faith.

AMANDA HELD OPELT
Speaker, songwriter, and author of *A Hole in the World*

This book is a splendid resource for anyone who is interested in pursuing the Christian life more intentionally. Paul Gutacker's humble, conversable voice makes the book a delight to read. Like A. G. Sertillanges' famous guide *The Intellectual Life*, this book shifts effortlessly from the sublime to the very practical—from the theology of St. Athanasius to how to host a dinner party. It's a wonderful read.

ELIZABETH COREY
Honors Program Director, Professor of Political Science,
Baylor University

The answer to our lament over the loneliness and isolation of our current culture is creating space for deep Christian community. That's what Brazos Fellows does, and it does so with intellectual vigor, religious devotion, and a passion for beauty. In this book, Paul Gutacker shares the story of this fellowship. Like a boot camp for the soul, Brazos Fellows refines those in its communion through carefully curated reading, focus on spiritual practices, and friendships that will last a lifetime.

JESSICA HOOTEN WILSON
Fletcher Jones Chair of Great Books at Pepperdine University

Practicing Life Together

A Common Rule for Christian Growth

PAUL J. GUTACKER

MOODY PUBLISHERS
CHICAGO

© 2025 by
Paul J. Gutacker

All rights reserved. No part of this book may be reproduced in any form without permission in writing from the publisher, except in the case of brief quotations embodied in critical articles or reviews.

Scripture quotations, unless otherwise indicated, are taken from the Revised Standard Version of the Bible, copyright © 1952 [2nd edition, 1971] by the Division of Christian Education of the National Council of Churches of Christ in the United States of America. Used by permission. All rights reserved.

Scripture quotations marked (ESV) are from the ESV® Bible (The Holy Bible, English Standard Version®), © 2001 by Crossway, a publishing ministry of Good News Publishers. Used by permission. All rights reserved. The ESV text may not be quoted in any publication made available to the public by a Creative Commons license. The ESV may not be translated in whole or in part into any other language.

All emphasis in Scripture has been added.

Quotations from the *Book of Common Prayer* are taken from the 2019 edition, copyright © 2019 by the Anglican Church in North America.

Edited by Pamela J. Pugh
Cover and interior design: Charles Brock / Brock Book Design Co.
Cover element of leaves copyright © 2025 by filo/iStock (148016337). All rights reserved.
Author photo: Eric Guel Photography

ISBN: 978-0-8024-3518-7

Originally delivered by fleets of horse-drawn wagons, the affordable paperbacks from D. L. Moody's publishing house resourced the church and served everyday people. Now, after more than 125 years of publishing and ministry, Moody Publishers' mission remains the same—even if our delivery systems have changed a bit. For more information on other books (and resources) created from a biblical perspective, go to www.moodypublishers.com or write to:

Moody Publishers
820 N. LaSalle Boulevard
Chicago, IL 60610

1 3 5 7 9 10 8 6 4 2

Printed in the United States of America

To Paige, and the joy of our life together

Contents

The Trellis: An Introduction — 11

PART ONE
Gather: Learning to Be Together

   1. Breaking Bread: Life at the Table — 25
   2. Life Together: The Gift and Challenge of Community — 39
   3. Practicing Weekly Dinner — 55

PART TWO
Pray: Learning to Listen

   4. Speaking with God: The Life of Prayer — 71
   5. Keeping Time: Living in Rhythms of Prayer — 85
   6. Practicing Common Prayer — 99

PART THREE
Study: Learning to Wonder

   7. Loving the Lord with All Our Mind: The Life of Study — 115
   8. Our Inheritance: Receiving the Gift of Tradition — 129
   9. Practicing Reading Together — 145

PART FOUR
Discern: Learning to Attend

   10. Preparing to Die: Living Our Vocation — 161
   11. Hearing His Voice: The Lifelong Project of Discernment — 177
   12. Practicing Sabbath — 191

As We Close — 205

Further Resources — 207

Acknowledgments — 213

Notes — 215

Almighty God, you alone can bring into order the unruly wills and affections of sinners: Grant your people grace to love what you command and desire what you promise; that, among the swift and varied changes of this world, our hearts may surely there be fixed where true joys are to be found.

Collect for the Fifth Sunday in Lent, the *Book of Common Prayer*

The Trellis:
An Introduction

Last spring, the kids and I planted a garden. We're novice gardeners, but we like getting our hands dirty and we aspire to eat more vegetables. So, in great hope, we planted lettuce, kale, squash, and a variety of tomatoes. Then two things happened: Life got very busy, and Texas had an unusually rainy spring. Next thing we knew, we had tomato plants blooming and billowing out over half of our backyard.

As any actual gardener knows, tomatoes need a trellis—a stake or cage—to grow, or they'll end up turning into a tomato jungle. I knew this, but failed to install a trellis when we planted. Finally in early May, I tried to retroactively stake the tomatoes. The result? Bent cages, broken vines, and a very frustrated gardener. The late staking still helped, but we'd have had happier plants—and more fruit—if they'd grown on structure from the outset.

What's good for tomatoes is good for people. This is why, throughout the church's long history, Christians have recognized the benefit of a "rule of life."

A RULE OF LIFE

A rule of life is like a trellis. It's a standard, offering guidance and encouraging growth in the right direction. It's a way of living intentionally—of making a commitment to practices that should frame your life.

Unfortunately, when some people hear the word "rule," they think of legalism—a list of dos and don'ts we must follow to stay out of trouble. Rule connotes bondage, constraint, a lack of freedom. But these connotations are almost exactly wrong. Putting a trellis around your tomato seedlings doesn't suffocate them but encourages growth.

More precisely, the trellis encourages growth *in the right direction*. People, like tomatoes, are going to grow whether they have a trellis or not. The question isn't *if* we're growing but *toward what end*? When I left our tomatoes for over a month without a rule, they weren't static. They took shape, put down roots, and expanded—but not in ways most conducive to fruitfulness. Their misshapen growth could only be corrected with difficulty and pain. Straightening them back into the right shape meant losing more than a few vines.

We're growing in a direction too, whether we mean to or not. Our lives are shaped by countless choices, habits formed over days and weeks until they become grooves. Only with difficulty do we divert from the rut we've formed. And this is why certain times of our lives feel so weighty. All too quickly, before we even know it, our lives resemble a tangled, chaotic mess—a tomato plant taking over the yard.

THINK LIKE AN ATHLETE

And to be honest, most of this mess starts within. If you're like me, you know that our problems arise from our disordered desires—we want the wrong things, or want trivial things too much, or don't want the best things enough. And even when we desire good things, we often fail to follow through. Both our desires and our wills are not what they should be. The apostle Paul knew this all too well. "I do not do the good I want, but the evil I do not want is what I do," he laments to the church in Rome. His confused experience arises, he writes, from remaining "captive to the law of sin which dwells in my members" (Rom. 7:19, 23). Left to our own devices, to our whims and impulses, we find ourselves enslaved.

The Trellis: An Introduction

This is why a rule of life is so helpful. My tradition, the Anglican Church, describes it this way: "A rule of life is a discipline by which I order my worship, work, and leisure as a pleasing sacrifice to God." Why is this needed? The Anglican Catechism continues: "I need a rule of life because my fallen nature is disordered, distracted, and self-centered. A rule of life helps me to resist sin and establish godly habits, through which the Holy Spirit will increasingly conform me to the image of Christ."[1]

Paul would have agreed. If our disordered desires hold us captive, then freedom, paradoxically, comes through discipline. It's another misunderstood word: We think of discipline as a synonym for punishment. Like "rule," discipline seems to be all about coercion and restraint—things we think keep us from being our authentic selves. Or so we think.

Not Paul. In fact, right after waxing eloquent about his freedom in Christ, he urges the church in Corinth to commit to a life of serious discipline:

> Every athlete exercises self-control in all things. They do it to receive a perishable wreath, but we an imperishable. Well, I do not run aimlessly, I do not box as one beating the air; but I pommel my body and subdue it, lest after preaching to others I myself should be disqualified. (1 Cor. 9:25–27)

Just as an elite athlete cares about nutrition, sleep, hydration, exercise, and training, the Christian is called to the same kind of intentionality. And the athlete helps us see that discipline makes us *more*, not *less*, free. Who is more free to run a marathon? The runner who structures their life around a training regime, or the person who wakes up on the morning of a race and decides to give it a go? A disciplined life makes us more able to run. When we commit to a life of disciplines, we find ourselves less enslaved to our disordered desires. We're more able to say yes to the good and no to all that would pull us away.²

There's more to say about this countercultural understanding of freedom. But for now, the bottom line is what Paul assumed: The Christian life has a *telos*, or purpose, and our lives should be ordered toward that end with the same seriousness of an Olympic hopeful.

The Christian tradition calls this the *ascetical* life, from the word *ascesis*, or discipline. Today the word evokes a spartan existence with few possessions. But, in the church, it's a life of prayer, fasting, and self-denial. All these disciplines aim at strengthening us against the enemies renounced in baptism—the world, the flesh, and the devil—whatever the wording various traditions choose. Each discipline aims at our growth in the virtues of faith, hope, and love. To sum it up, ascesis is about growing in love of God and neighbor.

> **To sum it up, ascesis is about growing in love of God and neighbor.**

Following Paul's exhortation, some early Christians went to radical lengths of ascesis. With the determination and focus of an Olympian, spiritual athletes gave their lives to rigorous discipline. From Anthony the Great, who battled demons in the desert, to Simeon Stylites, who for decades interceded for the world from his perch on top of a pillar, these extraordinary ascetics inspired other Christians to join the race. A movement of Christian monasticism was underway.

Monasticism represented a renewed commitment to follow the teachings of Christ, no matter how demanding. But ascetics, and the communities that formed around them, were not an alternative to the church. They weren't a conclave of "super Christians" apart from the community of Christians. Instead, monastic life existed *for* the church. Not everyone became a monastic. But the laity and clergy alike were inspired by ascetics like Anthony who embraced poverty, solitude, and prayer that they might run so as to win the prize.

MONASTIC COMMUNITY: RUNNING WITH OTHERS

A few years ago, my running buddy moved away. Overnight, it became much harder to wake up to run at 5:00 a.m. three times a week when nobody was banging on my door. Now I can divide my closet between "the size that fit when Cody lived in Waco" and "sizes I had to buy after Cody moved." What I learned the hard way was a lesson the church realized long ago: Most of us benefit from running with others rather than alone.

Early on, the most famous way to be a monk was as a hermit—a life of nearly complete isolation and solitude. But even for hermits, monastic life was always relational and communal. Increasingly by the 300s, monastic communities invited believers to pursue the life of discipline together. Thousands of ordinary Christians, men and women alike, signed up. They were guided by wise teachers such as Pachomius the Great, who produced a plan for self-sufficient monasteries; Macrina the Younger, who taught her brothers how to integrate monastic ideals into the household; and Basil the Great, John Cassian, and Benedict of Nursia, who each wrote foundational "rules," or guides, for monastic life.

> Despite having a low view of monasticism, Protestants historically have recognized the vitality of practicing spiritual disciplines together.

The patterned communities that emerged from these rules—the Benedictine order, the Mount Athos monasteries, the Carthusians, and later the Cistercians, to name only a few—became training grounds for a rigorous Christianity. The longer story of Christian monasticism is wonderful, troubling, and too complex to detail here. Simply, these communities had an incalculable effect on the history of the church.[3]

Historically, most Protestants have had a low view of monasticism. Even so, Protestants have recognized the vitality of practicing spiritual disciplines together. From Lutheran "small groups" in the early 1700s to Methodist societies a few generations later, Protestant churches have been nourished by intentional communities of practice—communities that bore some similarities to monasticism.

More recently, Protestants have been more open to learning from monastic life. As the West becomes increasingly post-Christian, some see in monasticism a model for forming robust, resilient faith. Thus, recent calls for Christians to embrace "the Benedict option," or the Franciscan, or Trappist, or Pietist options.

Every Christian should live like a monk. That's what Greg Peters argues in his book *The Monkhood of All Believers*, explaining that the monastic aims to orient every part of their life toward "the one thing needful." Such single-minded devotion, Peters concludes, is in fact the vocation of every believer. We're all called, in this sense, to be monks.

Peters isn't alone, as many recent books and podcasts have encouraged evangelicals to consider taking on a rule of life. As *New York Times* columnist Tish Harrison Warren put it in her January 2023 newsletter, "This Year, Try Organizing Your Life Like a Monk."

This renewed interest in a ruled life is encouraging. But the retrieval can go one step further.

The title of this book riffs on a book of far greater significance: *Life Together*. Written by German theologian and pastor Dietrich Bonhoeffer, *Life Together* is a beautiful, realistic, and challenging book. Its thesis? For the Christian, community isn't optional. We need one another to hear God's Word, to grow in prayer, to grow in holiness. Bonhoeffer lays out a compelling vision, describing how prayer, table fellowship, and study make a life together.

Reading Bonhoeffer convinced me of something: A rule of life is good, but it's even better together.

How? What's the value of living by a rule *with others*?

What would it look like for ordinary Christians, outside of the cloister or the seminary, to commit to a common rule together?

LIVING BY A COMMON RULE

My own experience of feeling stuck after college eventually led my wife, Paige, and me to launch an experiment in Christian community. In 2018, we invited recent college graduates to come join Brazos Fellows, a community of men and women that prays, studies, and eats together. We began Brazos Fellows with the hope that this rhythm of shared life would help recent grads discern what to do. And while the fellowship mostly attracts emerging adults roughly twenty to thirty-five, over the years we've realized that the invitation Brazos Fellows makes—to live by a common rule—isn't just for those in this general age range. One reason we've realized this is that most years we've been joined by someone older. What's more, we've included in our community people in very different seasons of life—from middle-aged professionals to empty-nest moms.

> Rather than "What am I going to do?" the most important question is "Who am I going to be?"

I've come to realize that the question that fellows often come with isn't the best question. As we worked with fellows in discerning, it became clear that one's vocation can't be reduced to career. Instead of "What am I going to do?" the most important question is "Who am I going to be?"

These are questions we've been living with since Brazos Fellows launched in 2018. The fellowship invites college graduates to take on a common rule for an academic year. Fellows live in a rhythm of study, prayer, and work, all aimed at growing in knowledge of God and knowledge of self. They commit to particular practices (you can find our Rule at the end of this book) in the hope that doing these things together helps them become who they're meant to be.

For many Brazos Fellows, the Rule was the leading reason they applied. They wanted to commit to spiritual disciplines, including daily morning and evening prayer, Sabbath practice, and spiritual direction. They wanted to know that every day, every week, they'd be doing these practices. Regardless of what's going on or how they feel, they've committed, so they do them. Like a trellis, the rule provides structure and stability—it helps orient us upward, pointing us in a good direction for growth.

After nine months, they develop habits that stick. They've lived something like a monastic life, and want to keep at it. Recently, we surveyed alumni who were at least one year removed from the program. We wanted to see how many of them were still doing the things we did together. So we asked which practices remained "an important part of their Christian life," and here's what they said:

- 100 percent said that liturgical prayer remains important.

- 100 percent answered the same about Christian community (90 percent attend church at least weekly, with 70 percent serving or leading in their local church).

- 90 percent said that Sabbath practice, confession, offering hospitality, and theological study each remain important.

- 80 percent continue in spiritual direction.

That's the thing about a rule—if you commit to it long enough, it starts to stick. What we've watched happen with Brazos Fellows, year after year, is why this book exists. The book draws on our experience, distills some of the most transformative practices, and asks the question: How might others do something like this?

The pitch is that you, too, can live like a monk. Living by a common rule isn't just for vowed monastics—it offers ordinary Christians a structure for deep, lasting spiritual growth. And this structure might be particularly helpful for those of us figuring out adult life or during times of transition. In the chaos and isolation of post-college years, a common rule offers stability, accountability, and support; conversely, twentysomethings have the time, flexibility, and desire to respond to a "big ask." And not only emerging adults: As we go through life, we'll encounter transition, different times of self-examination, opportunities to reorient our practices.

THE BIG ASK: Here's the invitation I want to make to you: Commit to a common rule. Make an intentional commitment, with others, to spiritual disciplines that will shape how you grow and who you become. Practice life together.

HOW A RULE CAN BE A GIFT

When I talk with people, college students especially, about their walk with God, they tell me they're tired of trying to figure it out on their own. They share their struggles to regularly pray and read Scripture. They crave consistency and community. They want to commit, to develop spiritual habits that will stick.

If you can relate, you're ready to receive the gifts of a common rule. Let me name a few:

THE GIFT OF GRACE. A rule isn't something we expect to keep flawlessly—it's not another thing we "succeed" at perfectly. Rather, we commit to a rule because we know we aren't there yet. Failure, which inevitably comes, proves to be a gift when it chastens our pride and our sense of self-sufficiency. We embrace a rule, in other words, so that we can more readily and regularly hear the Spirit's call to repentance, God's invitation to turn once again toward the life He offers.

THE GIFT OF ORDER. For people, as for plants, structure is not antithetical but essential to life. In the beginning, God's Spirit brought order out of chaos, shaping a primordial mess into forms that allow life to come forth. What happened in creation also happens in new creation, when our new birth brings order out of the chaos of sin and death. By bringing order, a rule facilitates new life. And embracing a common rule embodies this hope—our hope not to live in slavery but in and by God's life-giving Spirit.

THE GIFT OF BELONGING. Growth also requires stability—it requires belonging. Belonging allows us to put down roots. When we take on a common rule, we know that we aren't going anywhere, at least for a season. So we put down roots that will help us withstand times of drought or storm. When we're part of a common rule, we don't face these challenges alone. We're held in place by a community bound together by the Spirit, who gives us gifts to sustain and strengthen each other.

THE GIFT OF FRIENDSHIP. Most good things are even better when they are shared. These "common goods"—such as prayer, a good meal, or an afternoon of rest—are enriched, not diminished, when we do them together. And when we partake of common goods with others, and do so over time, friendship grows. Put another way, a common rule offers soil in which friendship can deepen and flourish.

You might have noticed that these benefits of a common rule are ultimately due to God's Spirit. A common rule is not magical it doesn't "work" because we've figured out a technique. The gardener fertilizes, tills, plants the seed—and gives it a trellis. These don't *make* growth happens, but only support it. In the Christian life, the operative agent is the Spirit. A common rule creates space for the Spirit to work. And that space can be especially valuable as you're starting out after college. For those of you facing uncertainty, struggling to discern who you are, or wanting deeper friendships, a common rule is a gift. This book invites you to receive it.

"WHERE TWO OR THREE ARE GATHERED"

I had planned to write this book primarily with emerging adults in mind—people in those bridge years between college and being fully settled down. These are the sorts of people who tend to do radical things like move to Waco, Texas, to join a semi-monastic community. It turns out, however, that this idea isn't just a good fit for a "gap year."

It's not a stage of life but a way of life.

Whether you're a busy college senior, a recent grad, a mother of three, a high-schooler starting to look ahead, in the midst of a successful career or making a change, or even getting ready to start retirement, if you want to grow, keep reading.

This book invites you to ask others to commit to a common rule of life—to not go it alone in your bridge years or wherever you are in life. It's not a how-to book. It won't solve all the problems I've named above.

Instead, it's an invitation to four aspects of life together: community, prayer, study, and discernment. Each part of the book considers one of these disciplines. How are we changed when we gather around the table? What happens when we pray? What does it mean to love the Lord our God with our minds? How might someone attend to their vocation, their calling?

Each part then explores what changes when we do these things together. And finally, each part invites you, with others, to *try*. Gather for weekly dinners. Meet for common prayer. Read together. Practice Sabbath rest.

Plenty of other good things might be part of a rule of life. But our experience with Brazos Fellows makes us confident that these four provide a foundational structure: **EAT, PRAY, STUDY,** and **ATTEND TOGETHER.**

If all four sound daunting, perhaps one will stand out as particularly needed in your life right now. For a growing tomato plant, a trellis is very good, but a simple stake is much better than nothing. Those who can't train like Olympian athletes still benefit in the long run from a few quick workouts a week. Starting small is better than never starting at all.

Perhaps you're asking, But who will join me? What if my friends are already over-committed, or what if I find myself in a community mostly made up of unbelievers? Several undergraduate students read a draft of this book, and this was their biggest question: But how do I find people who would do this kind of thing with me?

The answer, again, is starting small. All you need is one or two people who are willing to commit to a practice for a year. In fact, a group that size might be best for trying out a common rule. After all, our Lord said, "Where two or three are gathered in my name, there am I in the midst of them" (Matt. 18:20).

If you find a few others, you could read and discuss this book together as an experiment in forming a common rule. Read a chapter a week for three months, or one part weekly and be done in a month. Consider it a trial period for a new common life together. As you're able, start some of the practices while you're reading. Meet one morning a week for common prayer together, and one evening to share dinner and discuss the reading.

As you read, and as you practice, try to discern what is most valuable for you and your community. Not everything in these pages will be for you. Ask the Lord to guide your reading, to help you hear what's most beneficial, and not to worry about the rest.

Gather: Learning to Be Together

PART ONE

Breaking Bread: Life at the Table

Life Together: The Gift and Challenge of Community

Practicing Weekly Dinner

O God, whose blessed Son made himself known to his disciples in the breaking of bread: Open the eyes of our faith, that we may behold him in the fullness of his redeeming work; who lives and reigns with you, in the unity of the Holy Spirit, one God, now and for ever. Amen.

Collect for the Wednesday of Easter Week, the *Book of Common Prayer*

1

Breaking Bread
Life at the Table

I assume that you, my reader, are embodied. You hold this book in your hands, resting an elbow on a desk or table, taking in the printed (or digital) page with your eyes. You, in other words, encounter this book as an embodied creature.

Let's take a moment to notice this basic fact: At the end of this sentence, close your eyes, and focus on your body for sixty seconds.

Okay. What rhythms did you feel? (Your eyes, I take it, are back open.)

Perhaps you noticed your breath, one of the most obvious rhythms, as you inhaled, exhaled, and repeated. As if to the beat of a silent metronome, your lungs draw in air and push it back out. Similarly, your heart tick-tocks, pulsing blood forward and back, inch by inch, through your veins. Your body is keeping time—it's in rhythm.

We could name many other rhythms. Your eyes blink, again and again. When you speak, you do so in a rhythm of sound and silence. Several times a day, smell and taste work in tandem to awaken and focus hunger, helping you replenish your body with food. Every evening, fatigue starts to shut your body down—not all the way to the unconsciousness of death, but something strangely like it. Every morning, you return to wakefulness.

Moment by moment, day by day, we live in rhythm. We live in a world of order and patterns and find our bodies in step with these rhythms. If the natural world is ordered by seasons, by cycles of renewal and decay, growth and death, likewise so are we. Put another way, all that we discussed in the previous chapter about the passing of time is experienced in our bodies. You might say that our bodies are "timed," or perhaps that we embody time.

Yet, if our embodied existence is meant to be in rhythm with an ordered world, it often struggles to keep the beat. Our intentions, our desires, so often seem out of step with our bodies. Our experience of time feels fragmented and incoherent. We weaken, we fatigue. We nod off when we mean to be alert; we lie awake when we wish to be asleep. We fidget, bounce, tense up. We struggle to focus, our minds wander, we think ahead. We forget things we mean to remember. We can't stop recalling something we'd rather forget. We lose patience, we get irritable. We feel discomfort, itchiness, aches, pains. We experience much confusion in our bodies. The passage of time only seems to make it worse, as our bodies change, decline, and decay.

In his letter to the Romans, Paul laments the disorder we experience in our bodies:

> I find it to be a law that when I want to do right, evil lies close at hand. For I delight in the law of God, in my inmost self, but I see in my members another law at war with the law of my mind and making me captive to the law of sin which dwells in my

members. Wretched man that I am! Who will deliver me from this body of death? (Rom. 7:21–25)

In the next chapter, he names the longing we so often feel: "If we hope for what we do not see, we wait for it with patience" (Rom. 8:25).

Like Paul, we find ourselves fragmented, dispersed, scattered, pulled in different directions. Our bodies seem to be a real problem. Even now you might notice your bodily experience getting in the way of reading—that whatever fatigue, pain, hunger, or restlessness you presently feel seems to prevent you from immersing yourself in these words. It's difficult to bring all of who we are, body, mind, and spirit, to *attend*.

And if you're like me, these bodily distractions are especially noticeable when trying to pray. Precisely because of the discomforts and limitations of embodiment, I find it difficult to simply *be present*—to fully inhabit a moment. And prayer, as it turns out, only happens in the present. It would be tempting to conclude that I'd be better off, at least when it comes to prayer, if I didn't have a body at all.

Is this true? Is embodiment an obstacle to prayer?

Do our bodies only get in the way of our spirituality?

How do we deal with the confusion we experience in our bodies, the difficulties we have inhabiting time?

THIS BODY OF DEATH

One way of solving these difficulties is to say, yes, the body is a problem to be escaped. This "solution" was perhaps the most significant—and most dangerous—of the early Christian heresies: Gnosticism. In the early second century, Gnostic preachers made a persuasive argument: Isn't embodiment the root of all our problems? Don't our worst inclinations arise from bodily shortcomings, bodily desires? Wouldn't our souls be free to pursue the Good, the True, the Beautiful, if they were rid of all the messiness, all the distractions, of the body?

The church quickly recognized that this ideology failed on several counts. Gnosticism denied the goodness of creation; what's more, it couldn't fit with the central Christian claim about Christ: that in Jesus, God took on human flesh. (Some Gnostics, for example, taught Docetism, or the notion that Jesus only *appeared* to take on human form.) Against the Gnostics, the church fathers vigorously defended the goodness of the body.

The witness of the early church is clear: Neither our bodies nor our finitude are design flaws. We were made to be embodied creatures. What's more, our bodies are destined for resurrection. Put another way, the spiritual life is not about ignoring our bodies or escaping their limitations.

> Worship in the early church was very much embodied—it was remarkably *physical*.

In fact, when you look at the early church, you notice how worship was very much embodied—it was remarkably *physical*. Because "God is known in a human being who could be seen and touched," early Christians cherished material things, things that could be held, seen, tasted, smelled, including "water and oil, bread and wine, milk and honey, and salt, the bones of the saints . . ."[1] One can hardly read about early Christianity and think that the church disdained materiality, though the mention of bones can sound freaky to us!

But even while affirming the goodness of the body, Christians recognized its difficulties. Our time-bound, embodied existence is God's design; we also experience it as broken, confused, marred by sin. So early Christians paid a great deal of attention to questions like these:

How are our bodies—with which we hunger, desire, grow weary, enjoy the comfort of embrace—involved in our spiritual life?

What gives shape and order to our experience of being embodied in time?

How should we discipline our bodies?

All of these questions came together around a rather everyday matter: food.

FEEDING, FASTING, AND FEASTING

Food plays no small part in the drama of God's people. The Hebrew Scriptures are replete with stories, guidelines, laws, and restrictions on when and what to eat. And Jews and Christians aren't unique in seeing food as spiritually significant. You'd be hard-pressed to find a religion or culture that doesn't include rules for eating.

That's because our way of eating is distinctively human. As Jewish philosopher Leon Kass notes,[2] there's something unique about human posture that shapes our eating. Animals approach the world oriented toward consuming it. They are effectively a tube—a hole on one end takes food in and a hole on the other expels waste. As animals move through the world horizontally, their vision shares the same line as their feeding tube. Think of a giant whale shark swimming through the ocean with its mouth gaping open—this is the orientation of four-legged animals. What they see is what they eat.

By contrast, Kass observes, humans have an upright posture. We don't move through the world as a consuming tube; our sight is perpendicular to our feeding hole. We see, decide, then eat. We have the ability to discern, to judge, to make moral and ethical deliberations about our feeding. And this explains the ways in which human eating is both alike and different from other creatures.

All animals feed—all consume other life in order to live. But, Kass points out, only humans feast and fast. Only humans deliberately go without food for a time, withholding from ourselves what we need; only humans feast, going to great lengths to make meals much more elaborate and costly than is necessary. While humans eat because we must, we also do more and less than survival would dictate. And this seems to be universal—virtually every culture has its own set of feasting and fasting practices.

This insight of Kass's raises many questions. But first I must acknowledge that food isn't easy for many of us. Our relationships with food may be troubled by illness, allergies, and eating disorders. We may eat too much, or not enough, or lack access to healthy food. In a fallen world, we can't talk about feasting or fasting without talking about injustice, exploitation, and malnutrition. To one degree or another, each one of us has an imperfect relationship with food. We need to recognize this even while exploring the goodness and spiritual significance of eating.

How does it matter that humans are meant for more than just consuming in order to survive?

How might feasting and fasting require each other? How might they be two sides of one coin?

How might fasting help us avoid endless consumption and overindulgence?

How might feasting differ from gluttony? How might it correct a utilitarian approach to food, and thus to life?

And, to return to our bigger question about being embodied creatures, what, if anything, does our feeding, feasting, and fasting have to do with God?

RECOGNIZING GOD AT THE TABLE

Once you start looking for food in Scripture, you realize that meals are everywhere. In fact, it's rare to find a significant moment in the Bible that doesn't somehow involve a meal.

Consider: from Adam and Eve eating from the forbidden tree in the garden of Eden, to the Passover meal that precedes Israel's exodus from Egypt, to the heavenly manna provided them in the desert, to the widow whose oil never runs out, to Christ's first miracle at the wedding feast in Cana, to the risen Lord cooking breakfast on the beach for the disciples, to the wedding feast of the Lamb in the book of Revelation. If you took a few minutes, you could think of dozens (hundreds?) of other examples of meals in the Bible.

The Bible gives plenty of instructions about food too: from Leviticus to Deuteronomy to the book of Acts to Paul's instructions in 1 Corinthians. One could write entire books on allusions to food in the Psalms, or food in the Song of Solomon, or food in the Prophets, or food in Christ's parables. (Think of the lists you could make about thirst, water, wine, honey, oil, salt, grapes, milk, and so on in Scripture.)

Obviously, we can't possibly sum up all the ways in which food is significant in the Bible. But several themes are worth noticing.

First, meaningful things happen at the table. From start to finish, the story of Scripture is a story of eating. You might even go so far as to say that the story of God's people happens around the table. This is what you'd expect if Kass is correct, and our eating is profoundly connected to what it means to be human. And it's what we see throughout the Bible.

Second, to understand who God made us to be, we should consider our eating. The Bible doesn't give us a dietary plan. God's specific intentions for what and how we eat aren't entirely clear, especially since Scripture itself revises for Christians what had been expected of Israel. But it would be hard to read Scripture and come away thinking that our eating is spiritually insignificant.

So what's the significance of eating? What might we learn about ourselves and our relationship to our Creator from Kass's three kinds of eating (feeding, fasting, and feasting)?

Feeding reminds us of our complete dependence on God's

generous provision. We can't live without food. Our life continues because God has graciously made a world of abundant provision, a world with rich soil, sunshine, and rain, teeming with plants and animals that in turn give us life. Feeding reminds us that our existence is an ongoing gift.

Fasting teaches us that we live "not on bread *alone*." Our need for physical sustenance is real, but it pales in comparison to our need for God. When we voluntarily choose hunger for a time, or temporarily abstain from certain foods and drinks, we recall that our deepest hunger, our truest need, is for God.

Feasting reminds us that God has made us to share in His joy. Our redemption isn't just about getting out of the punishment we deserve. It's about so much more. This is why the end of the story is a wedding feast—a great celebration.

Third, gathered around the table, we become a people. You'll notice that most of the food-related stories cited are not about individuals. Many are stories of hospitality, of welcoming strangers, of God's provision for a community, or a family. This is why our common rule starts at the table: "We are what we eat," but also, we might add, "We become who we eat with." For this reason, people were scandalized by those whom Jesus was willing to join around the table. And this is why the early Christian community wrestled with similar questions: Who is welcome to pull up a chair? Who can sit with whom? What can and can't we eat? Who gets to eat first? These questions mattered because communities are formed around the table. It's where we learn who we are, where we belong, and what it means to be an "us."

Fourth, we come to recognize Christ across the table. Throughout the Gospels, Jesus frequently surprises people with His table manners. He doesn't eat, drink, or generally behave in ways that people expect. He eats with the wrong people. He provides the best wine when any old wine would do. He acts like a servant, washing the disciples' feet.

He orders the disciples to feed a huge crowd without adequate provisions. He walks through walls and then eats a bit of fish to prove He's not just a spirit. He endorses Mary sitting at His feet instead of working as hostess. Again and again, Jesus subverts people's expectations at the table.

Often, it's at the table where we learn who Christ is—where we see what God is like. It's at the table where He serves us, where He plays both host and servant. It's at the table where we betray Him. It's at the table, thanks be to God, where He restores us.

And we see all of this around one particular table, in one particular meal: when Christ gives bread and wine to His disciples, and tells them to partake of His body and blood.

What happens at the Lord's Table? What's going on in Holy Communion?

How does this meal show us not only who Christ is but also what it means to be human?

How does this meal relate to becoming a people—being a community?

COMMUNION: EATING THE BODY, BECOMING THE BODY

I grew up in a church tradition that saw the Lord's Supper as a memorial—a chance to remember. Celebrated four times a year, Communion was always somber and quiet. I approached Communion as a time for personal introspection—it was about me and Jesus. Communion gave me a moment to reflect, while holding my individual plastic cup of juice and piece of bread, on my sin and Christ's work on the cross. Indeed, in 1 Corinthians 11:27–29, Paul reminds us that we are to examine ourselves and not eat the bread or drink from the cup "in an unworthy manner."

I'm grateful for my experience in the churches I was raised in. But I've come to learn that there's more to Holy Communion. Both Scripture and early church theologians present Communion in *corporate* terms. In fact, the word *corporate* comes from the Latin *corpus*, or body. Let me explain.

In his epistles, Paul insists that what it means to be a Christian is belonging to Christ's body. This theme is especially strong in his letter to the Ephesians, where Paul writes that Christ and the church have been mystically joined—the two "become one flesh." In some mysterious way, the church *is* the flesh of Christ. Christ is the head, we are the body. So far, so good.

But just when you think you know what Paul means by "body of Christ," he uses it in another sense. In 1 Corinthians 10, he writes, "The bread which we break, is it not a participation in the body of Christ? Because there is one bread, we who are many are one body, for we all partake of the one bread" (vv. 16b–17). In the following chapter, Paul gives us the words of institution: Christ "took bread, and when he had given thanks, he broke it, and said, 'This is my body which is for you'" (1 Cor. 11:23b–24). Wait, hold on, Paul. Now it sounds like "the body of Christ" means the eucharistic bread. So which is it?

Then, in chapter 12, Paul switches back: "For just as the body is one and has many members, and all the members of the body, though many, are one body, so it is with Christ" (1 Cor. 12:12).

What's going on? Why, in one breath, does Paul speak of the bread as the body of Christ, and in another use the same phrase to describe the church? How do these two different bodies relate?

The answer is simple: We become what we eat.

When we *receive* the body of Christ, given to us in some mysterious way in the bread, we are *made* into the body of Christ. When we eat the body, we become the body.

Once you see this, you can't unsee it, especially in the writings of Paul and John. And this same understanding of Communion was explicated by early Christian theologians from the Latin-speaking West to the Greek-speaking East: Cyprian, John Chrysostom, Augustine of Hippo, Athanasius, and more. Their view is summed up well by Cyril, bishop of Alexandria, in the early fifth century: "Through one body, [Christ's] own body, he blesses his faithful in the mystical communion, making them one body with him and among themselves.... For if all of us eat the one bread, all of us form one body. Division cannot exist in Christ."[3]

Other church fathers made the same connection between the body of Christ that we receive in Communion and the body of Christ that is the church. "What is the bread?" asks John Chrysostom, fourth-century archbishop of Constantinople. "The body of Christ. Not many bodies, one body. Just as the bread is made of many grains, but so united that the single grains disappear, although they indeed exist but without their differences being seen because of their cohering, so we cohere with one another and with Christ."[4]

What's the point? Communion *makes the church*. Communion heralds our joining to Christ not as separable individuals but by incorporating us into His body. Communion with Christ necessarily means communion with each other. When I receive the bread and wine, it's not just about "me and Jesus." It's about recognizing that we have become a new people.

This has all sorts of implications. Above all, it means that the Christian life, our life in Christ, is never alone. As theologian Jean-Marie Roger Tillard puts it, "The moment of the greatest intimacy with the Lord—since one becomes his body—is also that of the greatest solidarity with others."[5] Instead of living by and for ourselves, instead of self-sufficiency and self-absorption, we enter into a new mode of being, defined by communion, by giving ourselves to and for the other. In short, we become the humanity God made us to be.

When we come to the Lord's Table, we come as we are, with all sorts of difficulties and shortcomings. Often, we're distracted and tired, muddled or uncertain. In our own bodies, and in our communities, we feel fragmentation and confusion. We may feel lonely, misunderstood, heartbroken. To varying degrees, we feel alienated both from our own selves and from each other.

But our risen Lord prepares a table before us, serves as our host, and offers Himself as our meal. We, His guests, are transformed. We become what we eat, His body. And then every other meal is changed too, as each becomes an occasion for heartfelt thanksgiving to God and genuine communion with each other. Every other meal is fulfilled in, and transformed by, Holy Communion.

What happens at the Lord's Table doesn't stay there. At the table, we commune with the Lord and with one another. We leave the table as a community, as a body. We go forward to live out our shared life—a life constituted by each other.

What should this life look like? What characterizes this community?

O God, you manifest in your servants the signs of your presence:
Send forth upon us the Spirit of love, that in companionship with one another your abounding grace may increase among us; through Jesus Christ our Lord. Amen.

Prayer for Mission,
the *Book of Common Prayer*

2

Life Together
The Gift and Challenge of Community

Just over a year after we married, Paige and I moved into a community house with five other friends. It was an exciting experiment. We were young, most of us newly married (three couples and one single friend), quite poor (having graduated in 2008, just when the economy crashed), and chock-full of ideas and enthusiasm.

The question that launched our experiment was, "What can we do together that we couldn't do apart?" We were sure that our year together would be transformative. We wondered how we might practice hospitality together. We planned on sharing the stuff of life—bills, groceries, prayer, downtime. We were very optimistic. Maybe the year would go so well we'd sign up for more—maybe for life.

Our year was fun, rich, and deeply meaningful—and unexpectedly hard. Community, we learned, is at the same time a gift and a challenge.

GIFTS AND CHALLENGES

That year held so many gifts. We shared meals and took turns cooking. We hosted fireside conversations, comedy nights, and international missionaries. Twenty college students camped on our floors when a winter storm kept them from going on retreat. We learned how to pray the Daily Office, waking up at what felt like the heroically early hour of 8:00 a.m. to pray from Phyllis Tickle's *Divine Hours*. We knew and were known more deeply during our year together.

There were also many challenges. We found it hard to balance time together with time apart. We bumbled through shared chores, struggling to collectively manage a household. We faced financial ups and downs, unexpected illnesses, and difficulties at work.

We slowly realized that we each brought with us very different expectations and hadn't set up structures for honest conversation and evaluation. Unsurprisingly, things started to fall apart halfway through the year.

> Community is always a gift. But it's a gift that challenges us.

We'd hoped that our year together would be an amazing success—a powerful testimony to why American Christians should abandon their individualism and all live in communes! Alas.

Yet, thanks be to God, the year was not a disaster. Our friendships emerged not only intact but deepened. We learned much about community, and about ourselves—the fears, anxieties, and hang-ups we'd brought to our shared life. It was a year of growth.

Community is always a gift. But it's a gift that challenges us. It's a gift that gives life, and heals; it's a gift that wounds, that can be painful.

This whole book is about life together, because a common rule is a fantastic way to form deep friendships and build community. But what characterizes a genuine Christian community?

What sorts of commitments, what ideals, are foundational for life together as Christians?

And how do we maintain these ideals—that is, live out this profound theological vision for community while being realistic about how this is *hard*? That community is both a gift and a challenge?

LISTEN CAREFULLY, MY SON

In the year AD 500, a discontented twenty-year-old decided to drop out of school. It's a story as old as time—but perhaps with atypical motivations. Born to nobility, raised a hundred miles from Rome, he was sent to the great ancient city for a proper education. Deeply troubled by the immorality of Roman society, he concluded he had to leave the city. He abandoned his studies, left the metropolis, and, while traversing a rugged and rural province, happened across a hermit. Inspired, he took up the solitary life, residing for three years in a cave. His life as a hermit ended when a local monastic community came and begged him to take leadership as their abbot.

The young man's name was Benedict—and what followed would reverberate through church history.

Benedict's first experiment in Christian community, as abbot of this monastery, was a disaster. The monks were disorganized, undisciplined, and didn't like Benedict's approach. Things got so bad that several monks tried to poison him! He took this as a sign to get back to his cave, where visitors continued to seek healing and guidance. Then an envious local priest tried to poison him; when this failed, he attempted to seduce Benedict with prostitutes. It was, to put it lightly, a rough start for Benedict living in community.

But Benedict was undaunted. Opposition and rivalry didn't keep him from working hard to bring others into the monastic life. By the time he left Subiaco, around AD 530, he had founded twelve monasteries in the area. He then went to Monte Cassino, southeast of Rome, where he founded a community that persists to this day.

Around the same time, he was hard at work on an even more enduring project: a set of principles to guide the life of the monastery that's come to be called the Rule of Saint Benedict.

SIMPLIFYING THE RULE

Benedict was familiar with other monastic rules, including the Rule of Saint Basil (the guide for monasticism in the East) and one simply called the "Rule of the Master," the most significant source for his own work. But Benedict didn't want to simply reproduce them. Decades of experience had taught him about the realities of Christian community. Above all, Benedict wanted to simplify the rule and adapt it to better care for the "weak monk." In the Rule of the Master, obedience to the abbot was a nearly impossible ideal. In Benedict's Rule, obedience was made "easy for anyone with a serious intention." The result became the standard Rule for Western monasticism.

How does Benedict's Rule begin?

"Listen."

This opening word was no accident. For Benedict, the monastic life is all about learning to listen: first and foremost to God, but also to the abbot, one's spiritual father. The first lines go on, "Listen carefully, my son, to the master's instructions, and attend to them with the ear of your heart. This is advice from a father who loves you; welcome it, and faithfully put it into practice."

Any monk who lives by Benedict's Rule will tell you that listening is central. Much of their day is spent listening. Benedictine monk Hugh Feiss describes this:

> A life of listening—to Scripture, to the writings of the church fathers, to the abbot, and to each other—required of the monks certain fundamental attitudes: the humility of a creature seeking to live in the presence of his Maker, the receptivity of a disciple

"in the school of the Lord's service," and the silence of one who is slow to speak and ready to learn.[1]

Listening is where we begin in our life with God, and it's foundational to our life with each other. You might say that, for Benedict, Christian community starts when we learn to listen.

BONHOEFFER'S EXPERIMENT

About 1,100 miles from Monte Cassino and 1,400 years after Benedict produced his Rule, a young German theologian opened an illegal seminary in Finkenwalde. Much like Benedict before him, Dietrich Bonhoeffer believed that what the church needed most, as it strove to remain faithful during the Nazi regime, was pastors deeply formed by Scripture and prayer.

And, like Benedict's early experience of community, Finkenwalde could hardly be considered a "success." Many students didn't appreciate Bonhoeffer's innovative approach, and some quit because of his rigorous expectations for their prayer disciplines and their community life. After two years the seminary was shut down by the Gestapo; dozens of Finkenwalde students were arrested; only a few seminarians ever entered into church ministry.

But Bonhoeffer's experiment also produced an enduring work: *Gemeinsames Leben—Life Together*. Written at Finkenwalde, *Life Together* captured Bonhoeffer's vision of how the church can live out its call to be a "community of love." In it, the pastor-theologian calls Christians to shed their ideals of what community can mean for them—their selfish desires for what they can get from others—and embrace the real community given them by God.

THE FIRST SERVICE: LISTENING

Where does such a community begin? With listening.

"The first service that one owes to others in the fellowship,"

Bonhoeffer writes, "consists in listening to them. Just as love to God begins with listening to His Word, so the beginning of love for the brethren is learning to listen to them."[2]

To learn listening, Bonhoeffer required that the seminarians sit in silent prayer and meditation at key points throughout their day: before morning prayer services, after breakfast, and before their evening prayers. Some days, during the lunch hour, the seminarians ate in silence while listening to a spiritual reading.

None of this is easy. But Bonhoeffer knew that listening does not come naturally. He realized that what we're often doing when we think we're listening is actually a false imitation—we're really only pausing our own speech temporarily while the other takes a turn. This isn't true listening; it's impatient and inattentive. It's just waiting for someone else to stop.

Bonhoeffer worried that future pastors, in particular, were tempted to overvalue their words: "They forget that listening can be a greater service than speaking." In reality, people need a listening ear. Will they find this, Bonhoeffer asked, in the church? Pastors might be given to loquaciousness, to many "pious words," or "spiritual chatter." This produced deadly spiritual consequences: "He who can no longer listen to his brother will soon be no longer listening to God either; he will be doing nothing but prattle in the presence of God too."[3]

Genuine listening requires an inner stillness, a self-collection that allows us to fully attend to the other. Henri Nouwen, another wise spiritual writer of the last century, agreed with Bonhoeffer on this point. "To listen is very hard," Nouwen wrote, "because it asks of us so much interior stability that we no longer need to prove ourselves by speeches, arguments, statements, or declarations. True listeners no longer have an inner need to make their presence known. They are free to receive, to welcome, to accept."[4]

BECOMING LISTENERS

How do we learn to do this? To give our full attention to the other?

How do we become people who can welcome others with our listening?

Most of us won't learn listening over decades of vowed life in a Benedictine abbey, or in an illegal seminary hiding from a totalitarian regime. But if Benedict and Bonhoeffer are right, we still have to ask these questions and learn these lessons. Listening is fundamental to every Christian's life. So even if we're not monks or seminarians, if we want to be a genuine Christian community we must become students of listening.

> If we want to be a genuine Christian community, we must become students of listening.

Learning to do this will be difficult—even painful. Likely, the path to such "interior stability" will take us through suffering. At a minimum, it will involve the loss of putting our own desires and needs first. It will involve the suffering of letting go of our hopes for an ideal community, and accepting the real one God has given us.

Listening in this way will also necessarily involve practicing a degree of technological asceticism—setting aside the distraction of screens. If you're serious about taking on a common rule with your friends, you'll want to ask questions like: What media and social media practices should we forgo so we can be present with each other? When and where do we need to ban phones?[25] What do we need to say no to so we can hear each other?

Let's consider some steps we can take, some other ways we can learn to listen.

Hospitality: Giving and Receiving

One way to learn listening is through a second fundamental practice—hospitality. Henri Nouwen closely connected the two: "Listening is a form of spiritual hospitality by which you invite strangers to become friends, to get to know their inner selves more fully, and even to dare to be silent with you."[6]

In addition to spiritual hospitality, Christians have always practiced tangible, physical hospitality. Why? Because we are those who have received hospitality from God. Put another way, when we show hospitality, we act like God.

Creation itself is a grand act of divine hospitality, in which God makes a space suitable for humanity to thrive. The same God who created a home for us sustains us through His hospitality: "Thou preparest a table before me" (Ps. 23:5). In baptism, we are welcomed to the church as an honored guest: washed and cleansed, we are given new clothes, and welcomed to the table. In the end, we will be welcomed by the host who left us with a promise: "In my Father's house are many rooms; if it were not so, would I have told you that I go to prepare a place for you?" (John 14:2–3).

> **Christ teaches His followers to offer hospitality and also to receive hospitality.**

As the consummate Host, God calls His people to do likewise. The Pentateuch instructs Israel to show hospitality to outsiders and the needy: "If your brother becomes poor, and cannot maintain himself with you, you shall maintain him; as a stranger and a sojourner he shall live with you" (Lev. 25:35). Likewise, through the prophet Isaiah, God exhorts His people "to share your bread with the hungry and bring the homeless poor into your house" (Isa. 58:7). The patriarchs and prophets are clear: Hospitality is the offering, the spiritual discipline, that God most desires from us.

What we see throughout the Old Testament is emphatically repeated throughout the New. Christ teaches His followers to offer hospitality, especially to children, the poor, and the stranger. Likewise, the apostles Paul and Peter repeatedly instruct the church to practice hospitality. In several places, hospitality is listed as one of the requirements for being a church leader.[7]

But Christ and His apostles also *receive* hospitality. Jesus is welcomed by Levi, by Peter's mother-in-law, by Zacchaeus, by Mary and Martha, by the disciples in Emmaus. Why is Christ so often the guest? We tend to think that I, the host, have something that you, the guest, lack. I give; you receive. We might even be tempted to say, for the scriptural reasons mentioned above, that the host is like God, while the guest is like needy humanity. But Jesus, the perennial guest, flips this around.

Christ shows us that it's often the host who is neediest—it is the host who needs transformation. Thus, in Matthew 25, Christ tells those on His right that when they welcomed the stranger, "you did it to me." By putting Himself in the story as the guest, Christ invites us to reimagine who has the greater need. While the stranger has clear, tangible needs—shelter, food, and rest—the host may have even more profound spiritual needs. Yes, the guest must find a place, but the host also wants a guest. Hospitality becomes an interchange of giving and receiving.

Hospitality reorients us, turns us away from ourselves, and opens us up to the other. Like Abraham, who receives God's promise when he welcomes the three strangers, when we open our door, we open ourselves up to God's transformative presence.

RISKING HOSPITALITY

So who is hospitality for?

Scripture prioritizes welcoming those who offer us no social or relational advantage—the child, the poor or the stranger. This is the richest, most transformative kind of hospitality, extended to those who will never reciprocate. In these radical forms of welcome, we bear witness to God's generous hospitality to us; what's more, as Christ says so clearly, when we do this, we welcome Him.

When we offer and accept hospitality, we lean into our true identity. We act like a body: each member interdependent with the other, each giving and receiving, in an ongoing exchange of generosity in which we do not seek benefit or calculate return. And, as we act like who we really are, we make more room for Christ.

As beautiful as this vision is, let's not sentimentalize it. We tend to imagine hospitality as a matter of beautiful tables and exquisite cuisine—something that will look great on Instagram. But true hospitality is risky. Welcoming the stranger is transformative in ways we can't possibly anticipate. Just as learning to listen involves loss and pain, welcoming someone opens us to unexpected joys and sorrows. The only thing we can be certain of, when we open the door or open our heart, is that we will be changed.

STABILITY: COMMITTING TO ONE ANOTHER

Neither listening nor hospitality is easy. But both seem pretty doable compared to the third pillar of Christian community: stability.

In the first chapters of Benedict's Rule, readers are warned about various kinds of monks who endanger a monastery. The worst kind of all? The "gyrovagues." Isn't that a great two-dollar word? Gyrovagues "spend their entire lives drifting from region to region, staying as guests for three or four days in different monasteries. Always on the move, they never settle down, and are slaves to their own wills and gross appetites." For Benedict, these are the worst possible monks. Even more than hypocrites or the morally lax, gyrovagues pose the greatest threat to monastic community.

Why is Benedict so hard on gyrovagues? Because genuine community requires *stability*. The antithesis to stability is spiritual tourism: never committing, never sticking with people, but going from one friend or group or church to the next. Like a butterfly, flitting from one flower to the next, taking what they can get from each, the gyrovague is not interested in the mutual growth and sanctifying possibilities of *staying*. Drop in, take what you need, and move on.

> **The antithesis to stability is spiritual tourism: never committing but going from one group to the next.**

Benedict's condemnation of gyrovagues is uncomfortable to hear today. Whether we like it or not, our world is characterized by change and flexibility, by high levels of mobility. Twentysomethings are much more likely to change jobs than their parents. If you're under forty, you're less likely to live in the same place, less likely to purchase a house, and more likely to move than the generation before yours.[8] You're much less likely to marry, with marriage rates now 60 percent lower than they were in the 1970s.[9] There's no single explanation for these dynamics. But the big picture can't be mistaken: We're less committed than ever to our professions, places, and people.

Even if we don't deliberately choose to be gyrovagues, mobility is still widely celebrated. Our songs and movies and advertisements show how much we prize our flexibility and "freedom." The stories we tell about what makes for a good life portray it as one free from binding commitments. Our cultural scripts encourage us to avoid being "tied down" or "locked in"—rather troubling metaphors for commitment.

So how might we recover the goodness of stability? And how might we make real commitments to community?

Practicing Life Together

For the Benedictine monk, stability isn't optional—it's one of the three vows taken by a novice. (The other two are fidelity and obedience.) The monastic life depends on being fully committed, for good.

Like Benedict, Anselm of Canterbury thought stability was a precondition for monastic life, describing it through the metaphor of the tree. He echoed Psalm 1's poetic account of the blessed man, who, according to verse 3,

> is like a tree
> planted by streams of water,
> that yields its fruit in its season,
> and its leaf does not wither.
> In all that he does, he prospers.

Anselm of Canterbury taught that the vow of stability allows one to put down "roots of love." Instead of the monk being dug up, transplanted, disturbed again and again, stability roots him firmly in one place. Only by putting down deep roots will the monk bear much fruit.[10]

> **Committing to one or two practices, with even one or two people, is a way of putting down a few roots.**

What could this mean for the rest of us? Whether by choice or necessity, we live more like tumbleweeds than trees. Even if we're drawn to Anselm's vision, how do we live this out? How might stability matter for those who won't ever make a lifelong vow—who won't commit to monasticism?

That question is, in some ways, the heart of this book's vision. I'm proposing the following: We move toward stability by committing to a common rule of life. Even if just for a season, a common rule makes us stable. Committing to one or two practices, with even one or two people, is a way of putting down a few roots.

And, if we choose this kind of commitment, we'll learn something that seems paradoxical: Stability gives us greater freedom. When we commit to each other, new possibilities emerge. We can know and be known in ways that wouldn't be possible if one of us ghosted next week, or moved on in a month.

We've seen this play out for the Brazos Fellows, who for nine months commit to a set of people, even if they wouldn't have naturally been friends. When things grow difficult, our commitment to our common rule becomes more important than ever. Things get awkward, someone feels wounded, our life together becomes a challenge, but stability makes it possible to find our way *through* rather than running away.

This isn't easy. To quote Rowan Williams, "The height of self denial, the extreme of asceticism, is not hair shirts and all night vigils, it's standing next to the same person quietly for years on end."[11] If we're really committed, it's going to be at a minimum uncomfortable. Sometimes, it might be devastating. In any case, it will be a gift.

Paige and I, and our friends, still think back on our year in community living and remember it with gratitude, laughing at absurd moments and enjoying good memories. We often reminisce and wonder, with wry chagrin, what we would do differently now.

When I think back on our community house, I'm grateful it dispelled a false notion: that real Christian community means no problems. I had this backward. Precisely because it was such a mix of joy and disappointment, embrace and struggle, our community was genuine. Together we learned better how to listen. Together we practiced hospitality, finding out that we were hosts in need, transformed by the ways in which Christ met us in the form of a guest.

Together we leaned in to stability, trying our best to be trees instead of tumbleweeds.

When we all finally moved out, we didn't graduate. These weren't lessons we wrapped up; we're still learning them many years later. Above all, we're learning them in practices, ways of being a community, that now make up the furniture of our week-to-week life. In particular, the practice of dinner.

Blessed are you, O Lord God, King of the Universe, for you give us food to sustain our lives and make our hearts glad; through Jesus Christ our Lord. Amen.

Grace at Meals,
the *Book of Common Prayer*

3

Practicing Weekly Dinner

One of my favorite scenes in Scripture is the Road to Emmaus. It's a story pregnant with meaning. It's a story about personally encountering Christ in entirely unexpected ways.

What was it like for those two disciples, before, during, and after they recognized their risen Lord? Remember the story with me: Picture them walking, fervent in conversation, and being joined by an unrecognizable Christ. Then, see them urging this shadowy figure—who is prepared to keep walking without them—to join them for dinner in their dining room.

What has changed? Their day began in sadness, as they walked the road lamenting: "We had hoped that he was the one." But as Christ illuminated the Scriptures, their sorrow slowly turned into a strange, bewildering hope. Now, they pull up chairs to the table, with no idea what is about to be revealed. We know what's coming next: "Their eyes were opened, and they recognized him." But not just yet.

Consider the Lord's patience with these two friends. He's spent the better part of a day with them. They are befuddled by grief, unaware of the great mystery about to be revealed. They not only don't know the great news, they can't even imagine it.

In the moment before Christ blesses and breaks the bread, picture the disciples leaning over the table, perhaps deep in conversation. He is about to open their eyes; for now, He is content to be present with them, keeping company. "He was at table with them," the apostle Luke simply puts it.

What does it mean to be "at table with" Christ? To be "at table with" each other? So many stories from Scripture take place around a meal. Why? Dinner together is the first practice of our common rule. What is the spiritual significance of something so familiar, so everyday, as dinner?

With the day mostly behind us, we take our seats for its final, most substantial meal. As I was growing up, my family enacted a typical liturgy around dinner: One of us gave thanks for the food, plates were passed, portions dished out (most likely spaghetti, or venison, or baked potatoes, always served with canned green beans). You couldn't leave the table until you recited the refrain, "May I please be excused? I am all, all done."

Nothing was more ordinary than this every-evening ritual. Only as an adult have I learned not to take these family dinners for granted. For many of us, dinner is eaten in the car after a drive-thru on the way home, or shoveled into our mouths while in front of the game or Netflix. And with young children, I realize why family dinner is rare. It's not easy to get children and food and parents all in the same place at the same time.

We know we lose something when we eat in front of screens. But what do we miss? What happens when, at the end of a day, we sit around a table together?

THE SPIRITUALITY OF DINNER

First, dinner helps us attend to the goodness of the everyday. Obviously we experience joy when we feast, when we enjoy an unnecessarily grand meal. And so we should! But a simple dinner, shared with others, also reveals God's goodness. Robert Capon, an Episcopal priest, wrote a delightful "theological cookbook" titled *The Supper of the Lamb*. Fr. Capon loves a good long feast—the book is all about throwing an epic dinner party. But he also reminds us, "Life is so much more than occasions, and its grand ordinariness must never go unsavored."[1] When we take the time to sit across a table, gathered over soup and bread, we celebrate the "grand ordinariness" of God's provision.

One of my favorite ordinary dinners happens in *The Lion, the Witch and the Wardrobe*. The famished Pevensie children are welcomed in by Mr. and Mrs. Beaver for a simple supper of freshly caught fish. C. S. Lewis describes the smell of the trout frying, the big melting lump of creamy butter, the sticky marmalade roll for dessert. Afterward, each leans back, cup of tea in hand, and gives a "long sigh of contentment."

All, of course, except for Edmund, who had recently been with the White Witch: "He had eaten his share of the dinner, but he hadn't really enjoyed it because he was thinking all the time about Turkish Delight—and there's nothing that spoils the taste of good ordinary food half so much as the memory of bad magic food."[2] Lewis puts his finger on the *sacredness* of an everyday dinner in good company—what makes it so satisfying to those hungry for goodness is the same thing that makes it unpalatable to a corrupted appetite.

Any dinner, even if not particularly special, still reflects God's grand purposes for all food: to sustain our bodies, to deepen bonds of belonging and fellowship, and to draw us into loving relationship with the God who provides for us. These purposes are especially and ultimately true in Holy Communion; they're also true of all our eating insofar as it is undertaken with generosity and gratitude. Dinner might not seem special, but that's the point: Because it's ordinary, it's worth noticing.

Second, dinner invites us to inhabit gratitude. Have you ever wondered where praying over meals originated? The practice goes back to ancient Israel. Following the teaching of Deuteronomy 8:10, "And you shall eat and be full, and you shall bless the Lord your God for the good land he has given you," the Jewish custom has been to pray after dinner. The traditional Jewish blessing translates to, "Blessed are You, Lord our God, Ruler of the universe, who brings forth bread from the earth." Likewise, the early church treated eating as an occasion for prayer, a time to sing our gratitude for God's provision.

One of my favorite saints is Basil the Great, fourth-century bishop and theologian. Basil is known for defending orthodox teaching on Christ, and for his beautiful writing on the Holy Spirit. But he also had much to say about dinner. And much of what he learned was from his sister Macrina. A deeply holy woman, Macrina wondered how the ideals of the desert ascetics might play out in an ordinary home. She translated monasticism into a kind of household asceticism, teaching her brothers to embrace a life characterized by "prayer, simple diet, and household work."[3] And, in turn, Basil taught others, preaching about feasting and fasting, and encouraging his congregants to live not for themselves but for others.

> If praying before meals seems basic, it's a sign we've become too comfortable. Have we become numb to God's daily provision?

Many of Basil's listeners would have experienced hunger themselves—a terrible drought in the area led to poor crops and a serious famine. In this context, it would be much more difficult to forget one's reliance on food. Every meal was an occasion for gratitude. As Basil told his church, "When you sit down to eat, pray. When you eat bread, do so thanking Him for being so generous to you. If you drink wine, be mindful of Him who has given it to you for your pleasure and as a relief in sickness."[4]

If praying before meals seems basic, it's a sign we've become too comfortable. Thankfully, most of us never feel true hunger. But have we become numb to God's daily provision? Feeding on the run, eating as multitasking, thoughtlessly consuming—these all make gratitude less possible. Praying together before dinner slows us down enough to give us the chance to notice that our life comes from God. And only when we notice can we be grateful.

Third, dinner reminds us that our life is shared. It's all too easy to think of ourselves as self-sufficient. All my experience of life is from my perspective—I'm in every scene, after all, so I must be the main character! I see my life as derived from and belonging to myself.

But the most basic fact of my existence is dependence. And this includes dependence on the lives of other creatures. Our life is sustained by consuming other life, both vegetable and animal. Sustenance comes to us through the work of farmers and fishermen and truck drivers and cashiers and cooks. In other words, our eating, just like all of our lives, is inextricably bound up with the lives of others.

If you want to undermine your illusions of self-sufficiency, the best way I know of is to eat with others. When we partake together in the liturgies of the dinner table—blessing, serving, passing, eating, washing up—we embody what's true about our life. "It is *our* daily bread that we eat," Bonhoeffer reminds us, "not my own."[5] When we sup together, we enact this truth. Most of us can't do this at every meal, but when we get to, we are given the grace to be a people. A good meal shows us that our lives are graced—they come to us as a gift.

And we not only remember, we also deepen these bonds with each other. Or, as my friend Jonathan Kanary, an Anglican priest, puts it, shared meals lead to shared lives, as the witness of the earliest church confirms (Acts 2:46). Spending time around the table makes us friends. Around the table, we become who we're meant to be.

So how do we do this? How do we open ourselves up to the transformation that can take place around the table?

LEARNING TO BE TOGETHER: RULES FOR THE TABLE

Your common rule starts around the table. But just because you happen to be sitting at a table with someone doesn't mean that you're together. If you've been out to eat anytime recently, you've seen it: a couple or a family sitting at a table while everyone stares at their phones. Obviously, this won't cut it. How can we be together, truly, over dinner?

Rules for the table are as old as human civilization itself. Every culture, everywhere, has expectations for what to do and what not to do when eating together. These vary wildly; for an introduction see Margaret Visser's delightful history, *Much Depends on Dinner*.

You'll want to come up with rules for your communal table, of course, but here are a few we've found helpful:

Rule #1: Be regular. If you want your dinners to build togetherness, to make you a people, then they can't be infrequent. If weekly sounds like a lot, remember that biweekly means that when someone has to miss, you'll go four weeks between all being together. We recommend weekly, and at the end of the chapter I'll give a few tips on how to pull this off.

> Whatever else you do, be sure to linger at the table.

Rule #2: Ban screens. This one should be obvious by now—but it's essential. There's nothing wrong with pizza and a movie, but that's not dinner together. Being together starts with being present. So turn off the TV, and put a basket by the door for people to leave their phones in when they arrive. Don't compromise. Commit: For the sake of company, we're staying off our phones for an hour or two.

Rule #3: Don't rush. Dinner together doesn't need to be fancy. In fact, it might help for it to be simple. Taking your time matters more than what you're serving. And, without being too fancy, you can extend a meal by breaking it into separate courses. First, sit down to cheese and wine, or another starter. Then, eventually, dish up a simple salad. Later, serve soup or a casserole. Finish with a slow cup of tea. What might have been served all at one time, and finished in twenty minutes, becomes a ninety-minute feast without too much effort or expense. Whatever else you do, be sure to linger at the table.

Rule #4: Everybody shares. At Brazos Fellows' weekly dinners we share "highs and lows." We go around the table and take turns, each telling about one high point and one low from their day (or week, or weekend, depending). Nobody gets left out, so it provides an easy opportunity for sharing if you're struggling or in pain. And it invites the rest of the group to participate in your joy or sorrow, to express love and care, and even to pray. Sometimes it's the occasion to celebrate something wonderful. In any case, it helps us know what's going on in each others' lives, without leaving anyone behind.

Rule #5: Do dishes. Life together makes a mess, and dinner isn't over until the kitchen is clean. Team cleanup is both easier and more fun—so make cleaning up part of your liturgy.

Rule #6: Go deeper. After dinner and dishes, spend time building understanding and affection for each other. Here are a few ways to do this (of course, depending on how long you take at the table, you can do some of these over dinner rather than afterward).

Share your stories. Every member takes an evening to share whatever they want about their life from birth to the present. We find it works well for the storyteller to share for about forty-five minutes. Afterward, others ask follow-up questions, before gathering around the person to pray for them. Don't start with story sharing on week one—take a month or so to build comfort and trust. And stress confidentiality; whatever is shared in these stories stays in the circle.

One way to form friendship is to "Bring a Thing You Love"—more or less "Show and Tell" for grown-ups. Everybody brings an object (e.g., book, photo, belonging, hand-me-down, artwork that they care about), and everyone gathered takes turns explaining why it's special to them. Do something similar with songs or poems. Know and appreciate each other by sharing in what people care about or delight in.

Pray together. Eating together and praying together go hand in hand. Unless there's another prayer activity (like praying for someone after their story), our community concludes with Compline, the five-minute service in the *Book of Common Prayer* for the end of day. It's the perfect way to draw our time to a close.

SAYING NO: FASTING AND ALMSGIVING

This chapter invites you to take up weekly dinners together as a practice. But each practice proposed in this book involves both affirmations and negations. You have to say no to something even as you say yes. In the case of food, the negation is fairly obvious: fasting.

Can we know the goodness of dinner without fasting? When we fast, we remember our dependence, experiencing our contingency, our helplessness. We feel, deep in our bellies, the emptiness of our delusions of self-sufficiency. When we break our fast, even a simple meal becomes delightful. In all these ways, fasting, surprisingly, affirms the goodness of creation.

This is why Basil, in his sermons on fasting, called Christians not to see fasting as some self-punishment or terrible burden to be borne, but rather to see it as a gift. Fasting, Basil explains, is like medicine to a sick soul. For those of us who are infected with the cancers of selfishness, consumerism, and self-reliance, fasting is exactly the medicine we need. He urges us to embrace the joy of fasting: "Run cheerfully to the gift of fasting."[6]

For Basil and Macrina, fasting was inextricably linked with care for the poor. They weren't alone; in their third-century sermons, Tertullian, Hippolytus, and Cyprian all instructed believers to fast so the church could provide for the hungry. In the second century, Aristides matter-of-factly pointed out that if there was no spare food, the church fasted for "two or three days in order to supply to the needy their lack of food."[7] Fasting, for the early church, often meant giving away one's dinner to the hungry.

Basil went even further. Inspired by Macrina, Basil gave away his fortune to care for the poor. He built the Basiliad, the world's first hospital—a place where travelers, the poor, and the aged might stay and receive free care. He organized a soup kitchen to provide daily sustenance to the hungry during a terrible famine and personally served up the soup himself. Following the teaching of his sister, Basil gave all he had—time and money—to care for others.

> We can take up ordinary ways of fasting and almsgiving.

I'm not sure how many of us will be like Basil. We should ask God if He's calling us to such radical generosity—He might. In the meantime, we can take up more ordinary ways of fasting and almsgiving.

Be like the early church: Fast once (or twice) a week. The early church fasted on Wednesdays and Fridays, with many Christians abstaining on these days from food and drink (except for water) until sundown. (Important caveat: Not everyone can do this, and some shouldn't. If you have an eating disorder, struggle with healthy eating habits, or have a physical condition that would prohibit abstaining from food, find another form of fasting.) If you're able to fast, consider giving away some grocery money to those in need, or to those working to alleviate hunger. Remember that you are needy, and feel your hunger for Christ.

Buy food for the hungry. My great-aunt Bernadine, a nun for over seventy years, told me about a simple practice of her monastic community: Every time they went grocery shopping, they bought one item to give to their local food bank or "blessing box." This practice is a little bit like the Old Testament injunction not to harvest to the very edges of the field, but rather to leave room for the poor to come and glean; it's also a sobering reminder of the abundance we enjoy.

Observe Lent. Lent is the season when, for forty days, the church follows Christ into the wilderness. Traditionally, Christians have embraced three Lenten disciplines: prayer, fasting, and almsgiving. Consider, as a community, taking up one practice in each of these three categories. Perhaps this could mean simpler communal dinners (go vegetarian, or abstain from desserts and alcohol). Consider skipping a meal to volunteer at a homeless shelter or soup kitchen.

Observe a fast from technology. If you want your table to be a place where friendship grows, ban phones from it. You can't be fully present—to the feast or to one another—if devices designed to distract are buzzing in your pockets. And you might want to go even further in your common rule. The more "screen time" you're willing to say no to, the more you'll be able to say yes to the common goods you're gathering around.

What would it be like to make fasting part of your communal rule of life?

What would be difficult for you, personally, in keeping a weekly fast? In what ways does this practice feel impossible?

What might those difficulties tell you about the assumptions, commitments, and values that structure your life?

And how might fasting be spiritually beneficial? How might

it deepen your dependence on God, your delight in God's good creation?

How might fasting make your feasting even sweeter?

GETTING STARTED WITH WEEKLY DINNER

Back when Paige and I lived in Vancouver and were both in grad school, we realized that although we had lots of casual friends, we needed community that was consistent. We needed friends we'd spend time with every week, regardless of how busy things got. So we emailed a few people we liked and asked if they'd be willing to commit to dinner together every Friday night. Thus, Friday Night Dinner Group (FNDG, for short) was born, and more than a dozen years later it's still going strong. Over the years, it's been a great gift, even as it's changed, morphed, and seen old friends move on and new friends arrive.

As an aside, if you find yourself in a new place or new job, and don't feel like you have yet made good friends, inviting others to be part of a weekly dinner for a season is a great way to build friendship. Find two or three people you'd like to get to know better. After three months of weekly dinners, you'll be well on your way to deep friendships.

What are some things to consider as you start practicing weekly dinner? How do you begin well with this part of your common rule?

Experiment until you find an evening that consistently works (hint: it's probably Friday). Our dinner group actually began on Mondays so everyone was free to do whatever they wanted on a Friday night. But we found Mondays tough with so much work looming. Then we realized many of the people we'd want to hang out with on Fridays were already in the group, and made the switch. We've found this worked great as grad students, and still does with a mix of young families and singles. Friday might not work for you, but we recommend trying it.

Find a home that works and always meet there. Another adjustment we made, about a year in, was to quit rotating locations. Changing the host meant lots of logistics and planning. Paige and I took over hosting, since our space fit the group and was centrally located, but everyone took turns cooking and bringing over dinner. Meeting in the same place provides consistency and removes a whole layer of planning, And, speaking as the usual hosts, I can say that it's pretty great for someone else to bring over dinner four out of every five Friday nights.

Keep the agenda simple. It's fine to do other things in your evening together: Discuss a topic, or work through a book, or watch an interesting series or show. But err on the side of keeping it simple. Life is busy, chaotic, and exhausting. It's nice to show up to dinner group knowing that the agenda is simply to eat and pray together, and that the evening's commitment will be just a few hours. Many (most?) weeks you'll be glad that's all that's going on.

Take breaks as needed. For our community we find that it works best to take summers off. During the summer, many of us travel, spend significant time with family, and get into different routines. So we find times to get together, but we intentionally step back from the weekly dinner schedule and then are excited to pick back up in August. (We take a similar break during the Advent/Christmas seasons too.)

When the two unnamed disciples sat down at their table—the stranger taking His seat across from them—they had no idea their lives were about to be forever changed. In a minute, as He blessed and broke the bread—"Blessed are You, Lord our God, Ruler of the universe, who brings forth bread from the earth"—they would go from despair to hope, death to life.

For those of us who partake in that resurrection life, our table gatherings can also be transformative. When two or three of us are gathered, Christ promises to be with us, and something as ordinary as dinner becomes a glimpse of glory—a foretaste of what is to come.

That's why, every Friday night, we stand in a circle and sing our blessing before the meal (to the tune of the Doxology):

> Be present at our table, Lord,
> Be here and everywhere adored,
> Abide with us and grant that we
> May feast in paradise with thee. Amen.

Pray: Learning to Listen

PART TWO

Speaking with God: The Life of Prayer

Keeping Time: Living in Rhythms of Prayer

Practicing Common Prayer

Almighty and everlasting God, you are always more ready to hear than we to pray, and to give more than we either desire or deserve: Pour down upon us the abundance of your mercy, forgiving us those things of which our conscience is afraid, and giving us those good things for which we are not worthy to ask, except through the merits and mediation of Jesus Christ our Savior; who lives and reigns with you and the Holy Spirit, one God, for ever and ever. Amen.

Collect for Proper 12,
the *Book of Common Prayer*

4

Speaking with God
The Life of Prayer

When did you learn to pray?

I can't remember a time in my life before I prayed. As an almost-three-year-old, I sat by my dad on a pond-side bench in rural Missouri and said "the sinner's prayer." Before every meal growing up, my family prayed a blessing over the food. I learned to pray as I learned to speak.

I'm still learning to pray. My prayer life has deepened and expanded, no question. I've come to love praying the Psalms. I've learned about the prayerful life from saints who've gone before. I've been blessed with friends and spiritual directors who have prayed with and for me.

But I still have plenty to learn. I easily forget to pray, or I pray with divided attention. Too often my prayers are shortsighted and selfish. Sometimes, if I'm honest, I treat prayer more like an item on my daily to-do list than an encounter with God. All this is to say that I'm not done growing in prayer.

Why is prayer often difficult? Why can it seem like a struggle?

Why do some people seem to experience God more in prayer than others?

What is prayer *for*?

Over the last few years, I've had the privilege of asking some of these questions alongside the Brazos Fellows. Every fall, the fellows spend a weekend in a beautiful retreat house on the edge of Texas Hill Country. In addition to long hikes and even longer meals, we spend the weekend praying and talking about prayer. For many years, my friend Nicholas, an Anglican priest and a professor of theology, led these retreats, and much of this chapter (including its title) is just me telling you things I learned from him.

And one of the things I've learned is that we need to learn to pray. Not just once—but again and again.

"TEACH US TO PRAY": ENROLLING IN THE SCHOOL OF PRAYER

Thankfully, we're in good company. In the gospel of Luke, the disciples see Christ praying, and what they see makes them realize their own deficiency. "Teach us to pray," they ask.

Christ's response to the Twelve is simple and short: He gives them a prayer.

Some Christians, skeptical about written prayers, have treated the Lord's Prayer, or the Our Father, as merely an example. It models the sorts of extemporaneous prayer we should invent for ourselves. But the majority of the Christian tradition has always seen the Lord's Prayer as more. It's not only a model but a powerful and transformative prayer that ought to be at the center of our prayer life.

Early Christian theologians saw the Lord's Prayer as a multifaceted jewel, a diamond you can turn this way and that so the light catches yet another angle. The Lord's Prayer, according to the early Christian theologian Tertullian, is "a summary of the whole Gospel."

Likewise, Cyprian, third-century bishop of Carthage: "How great, dearest brothers, are the mysteries of the Lord's Prayer, how many, how magnificent, gathered together in a few words, yet abundant in spiritual power."[1] Like a great poem, the Lord's Prayer is packed with significance—there's a density of meaning in every phrase, every word. Each petition can be unfolded, opened up, to reveal more of who God is and what we are to hope—and ask—for.

What can this prayer teach us? Let's join the disciples in the school of prayer. Let's look around and see who else is in class: several early Christian theologians, and one medieval mystic. With their help, let's learn some lessons from the Lord's Prayer.

LESSON ONE: PRAYER IS ALWAYS A RESPONSE TO GOD.

When we pray the Lord's Prayer we're praying words that God gives us. More specifically, we're praying words given to us by *the Word*, God's perfect revelation incarnate, Jesus Christ. In other words, like all prayer, the Lord's Prayer doesn't start with us.

Out of all the truths I've learned on prayer retreats with the Brazos Fellows, this is the most important. As my friend Nicholas put it, we never begin a conversation with God—prayer is always a response to God's address to us.

> Prayer isn't about me getting God's attention. It's not a skill I have to master before God will hear me.

What difference might this make?

For one, prayer isn't about me getting God's attention. It's not a skill I have to master before God will hear me. Instead, I can only pray because God has already spoken, He has chosen to reveal Himself, and the Word He has uttered has drawn me into a conversation I would never have started on my own. God has invited me into relationship. God starts things.

What's more, if prayer isn't a monologue *at* God but a dialogue *with* God, then it begins by listening to what God has already said. Left to my own devices, I usually kick off my prayers with a list of things I need or am worried about. What would change if I started with listening?

Hans Urs von Balthasar, a brilliant scholar and theologian, also spent much of his lifetime wondering about mystical experiences of God—he wondered about prayer, and those Christians who seem to go further in prayer than the rest of us. He concluded: "The better a man learns to pray, the more deeply he finds that all his stammering is only an answer to God's speaking to him."[2]

The first step in prayer is pausing to listen—to hear the Word that has already addressed me.

One of the church's great teachers on prayer is Teresa of Avila, sixteenth-century monastic, reformer, and theologian. At age sixty-two, she wrote a remarkable work on prayer, *The Interior Castle*. The book draws on Teresa's many years of living with, directing, and writing letters to ordinary believers who were hungry to experience divine love.

For Teresa, prayer begins by responding to God's call—His invitation to draw ever closer into intimate union with Him. And how do you hear this invitation? For the beginner, hearing God's voice usually isn't a matter of direct speech or supernatural experience (Teresa thought these were possible but more likely to come much later). In the early stages, God usually speaks to us through "words spoken by other good people, or through sermons, or through what is read in good books." God uses rather ordinary means like these—as well as "illnesses and trials"—to invite us into life with him.[3]

Teresa is wonderfully practical on this. If you struggle to get started in prayer, simply listen to what God is already saying. Prayerfully attend to what you've read in Scripture, what you've heard in sermons or a good conversation with a godly friend. *Listen*. Trust that the Spirit is praying in and for you. And then say something back.

LESSON TWO: PRAYER IS WHAT WE'RE MADE FOR.

So we want to hear and respond to God's Word. We've asked, like the disciples, "Teach us to pray." We've sat at our desks and opened our notebooks. And then our Teacher begins with this shocker: When you pray, say: "Our Father."

What?! These opening words should knock us over. Christ gives us a prayer that is His—He invites us to speak God's words to God. When you pray, writes theologian Rowan Williams, you should begin by "putting yourself in the place of Jesus."[4] What a privilege: to address God as if we were His Son. In Christ, we have been adopted, we are made sons and daughters of God—we now share in the special relationship between Father and Son.

Here's how Nicholas sums it up: Like all Christian prayer, the Lord's Prayer is a prayer to the Father, through the Son, in the Holy Spirit. When we pray it, we find ourselves welcomed into this triune fellowship. The words of the Son to the Father are now ours.

The intimacy of the Lord's Prayer didn't go unnoticed by the early church. Cyprian put it this way: "Imploring God in his own words, sending up to his ears the prayer of Christ, is a friendly and familiar manner of praying," he explains. "When we make our prayer let the Father recognize the words of his own Son."[5] In the Lord's Prayer, you name the truth that God has called you His child, made you His friend.

To be more precise, God has called *us* His children. The plural pronoun matters here: We address *our* Father, not *my* Father. The Lord's Prayer is communal. It's a "common prayer" in two senses: both a prayer that has been passed down and a prayer we pray together.

So just in its first two words, the Lord's Prayer has already taught us quite a bit. This is a prayer that rightfully belongs to the Son—and we get to pray it, together.

Practicing Life Together

And this reveals something rather stunning: In giving us this prayer, God welcomes us into His divine life. United to Christ, and partaking of the Spirit, God dwells in us, such that prayer is a participation in the loving communion of the Trinity. In prayer, we take part in that special relationship. We enter into that deep joy.

This is what we were made for. We don't exist because of some cosmic necessity or divine need. We don't fill up something lacking in God. Rather, we were created out of the overflow of triune love enjoyed in eternity by Father, Son, and Spirit. We exist because that love was so good, God delighted to make creatures that could share in it. As theologian Mike Foley put it, "God is a party, and you're invited."[6]

In other words, prayer is a foretaste of—a participation in—our *telos*, our final end. It's where we're headed.

Now at this point, someone sitting in the school of prayer might raise their hand. That one student protests: Hold on. This sounds great, but does it match what it's actually like to pray? If prayer is entering into the divine life of love, why doesn't it feel, well, divine? If it's what we're made for, why do we so often struggle to pay attention or fail to feel closer to God?

> Struggling in prayer doesn't mean you're "doing it wrong." Rather, difficulties are necessary for building our resolve.

For a long time I worried that the difficulty or dryness I experienced in prayer meant something was uniquely wrong with me. And then I read Teresa of Avila.

You might not think I'd get help from a sixteenth-century mystic. Teresa is most well-known for her experience of ecstatic union with God, which she narrated in blissful, even rather erotic terms (famously depicted in Gianlorenzo Bernini's *Saint Teresa in Ecstasy*).

What could such a person have to say to someone who gets distracted a few minutes into prayer?

But Teresa's decades of spiritual directing and praying with others left her quite realistic. While she has lofty expectations for prayer, she is also down-to-earth about the difficulties involved. In *Interior Castle*, Teresa writes that struggling in prayer doesn't mean you're "doing it wrong." Rather, difficulties are necessary for building our resolve—they help us grow in our intention to follow Christ. So don't worry about a lack of feeling. If you don't experience much comfort or consolation in your prayer—if, in fact, you experience spiritual dryness—this might be just what you need. It might help you grow in humility.[7]

Teresa helped me see that when I struggle to pray, it's not because prayer is unnatural or foreign to me but rather a reminder that I'm still on that journey of being restored to the person I was meant to be.

LESSON THREE: PRAYER TRANSFORMS OUR DESIRES.

Saying the Lord's Prayer with our young kids has reminded me just how basic it is. What do we need? Well, we need food. We need bread. It's a pretty ordinary request, and seems rather unnecessary, at least for middle-class Americans.

But even the prayer for daily bread, as simple as it seems, can be transformative. And it's transformative because, in prayer, the Spirit is uniting our hearts and minds to God, so that what we want and what we love is being conformed to what God wants and loves. How does that play out in this simple request? How does "give us this day our daily bread" invite us to be conformed to God's will?

Cyprian, writing in a time and place where food scarcity was a reality, and famine a real possibility, thought it was noteworthy that in the Lord's Prayer we ask only for sustenance. This petition teaches us to be content with our basic needs being met. A petition that seemed unnecessary from the comfort of my well-stocked home in fact poses questions: Am I content? Am I grateful for sustenance? Am I greedy for more?

But Cyprian's not done. He goes on to say that the "daily bread" petition calls us to imitate Christ by renouncing wealth and luxury. Only after this kind of renunciation can we genuinely pray for daily bread. Only after giving away his extra wealth will the Christian find himself relying on God's promise to provide everything he needs. Underneath the surface of this simple petition, there's a radical call: Leave behind luxury and follow Christ.[8]

Let me be honest: That's not a prayer I'm prone to say. Giving most of my money away, such that I would need to rely on God to provide tonight's dinner, is not something I naturally want. It's not something I'm going to pray on my own.

But, if Cyprian is right, as we pray the Lord's Prayer day after day, year after year, we might be changed. If we're open, we might be convicted about deriving a sense of security from our incomes and savings accounts. Over time, as we pray these words to the Father, through the Son, by the Spirit, we may be changed into people who want to be more generous—into people who desire to live on less and give away more.

> You know that you're growing in love by the increasing conformity of your will to God's.

Teresa spent her life working with women who had already done the radical thing described by Cyprian above—they'd renounced possessions and careers and embraced a life of prayer.

But that didn't mean they were done with transformation—far from it. Teresa worried that many of these dedicated monastics came to prayer looking for some sort of consolation, a feeling of closeness to God. This isn't a bad thing to want, but Teresa didn't think it was the point—even though she herself experienced rapturous moments of divine love.

The point of prayer, Teresa wrote, is *love*. And the way you know that you're growing in love is not a warm fuzzy feeling but rather the increasing conformity of your will to God's. Here's how she summarizes it: "It is in the effects and deeds following afterward that one discerns the true value of prayer; there is no better crucible for testing prayer."[9] Spiritual experiences are good, but even better? Transformation.

As we learn to hear God's Word, and as we respond in prayer, we should expect to be changed. But as soon as we say that, we need to clarify: That's not the only thing happening.

LESSON FOUR: PRAYER ISN'T JUST ABOUT TRANSFORMING OUR DESIRES.

Our outspoken classmate once again has his hand in the air. From the back row, he points out that it's starting to sound like prayer is about us accepting whatever God was already planning to do. So is that it? Is prayer just about us having a better attitude? We don't expect God to act differently—just for ourselves to feel different?

To be fair to our hypothetical questioner, these questions are serious. Maybe you've asked the same if you've ever prayed fervently for something—relief from chronic illness or depression, the gift of marriage or of children, healing for a desperately sick loved one—and not received what you asked for. Maybe it's best to

> **The God we meet in sacred Scripture is not the impersonal, unresponsive god of the Stoics, but a God who listens and responds.**

let God off the hook. Maybe our prayers were never about changing God's plan, but only about us learning to accept whatever was going to happen anyway.

This is a common way of coping with disappointment in prayer, and it makes some sense. The only problem? It's not how Scripture describes prayer.

In the Bible, prayer isn't about learning to passively accept our fate. The God we meet in sacred Scripture is not the impersonal, unresponsive god of the Stoics but a God who listens and responds. In fact, Scripture emphasizes this to a nearly embarrassing degree:

- In Genesis 18, Abraham begs for mercy on the righteous few in Sodom and Gomorrah. Six times he goes back to God asking for mercy for Sodom if fifty righteous could be found; he continues asking God to spare the city if forty, thirty, twenty, and finally just ten righteous are found.

- Exodus 3, where God puts it plainly: "I have seen the affliction of my people and I have heard their cries."

- Exodus 32 (ESV), when Moses pleads for the rebellious people of Israel: "And the LORD relented from the disaster that he had spoken of bringing on his people."

- Jonah 3, when the wicked people of Nineveh repent and call out to God, "and God relented of the disaster that he had said he would do to them, and he did not do it."

- James 5 (ESV): "The prayer of a righteous person has great power as it is working."

- Christ's promise in Matthew 7: "Ask, and it will be given you; seek, and you will find; knock, and it will be opened to you. For every one who asks receives, and he who seeks finds, and to him who knocks it will be opened."

Scripture seems completely uninterested in keeping our expectations low. The Bible is not nearly as worried as we are about hedging our bets. Over and over again, we are invited to pray and to expect that God will hear and grant our requests. As Tertullian boldly puts it, "Prayer alone conquers God!"[10]

In the Psalms, it's God's responsiveness to our prayers that leads us to thanksgiving and praise. "I will give you thanks, O LORD, with my whole heart," the psalmist writes in Psalm 138 (ESV), "before the gods I will sing your praise." Why? "On the day I called, you answered me; my strength of soul you increased." We pray to a God who hears, who stretches forth His hand, who saves.

And Psalm 138 doesn't contradict the other psalms that sound a note of lament. The reason the psalmist laments is precisely because God has not responded. It's because he prays to a God who hears that the psalmist also protests, entreats, cries out that things aren't as they should be.

Teresa had plenty of reason to lament. She lived with acute suffering and disability. Once, in her later years, she was traveling on a rainy, cold day to visit another convent. A wheel on her cart snapped off, and everyone and everything fell into the mud. Teresa loudly complained, "Lord, why do You have to make life so difficult?" As she tells the story, Jesus replied, "Teresa, this is how I treat My friends." "Yes, Lord," she retorted, "that's why You have so few of them."[11]

Being close to God doesn't mean keeping your complaints to yourself. God isn't interested in lowering your expectations. He wants you to ask and He promises to answer. But be advised: Part of God's answer might involve you.

LESSON FIVE: PRAYER INVITES US TO TAKE PART IN WHAT GOD IS DOING.

It's a little odd that in the Lord's Prayer we ask for "thy will be done, on earth as it is in heaven."

Doesn't God already want His will?

Doesn't God already know what's best?

So why bother? How in the world could our prayers change what God is going to do?

These theological (and philosophical) conundrums aren't new. They were wondered about by early Christian thinkers. I like how theologian Rowan Williams summarizes one way the early church answered them:

> God has decided that he will work out his purposes through what we decide to say and do. So, if it is God's will to bring something about, some act of healing or reconciliation, some change for the better in the world, he has chosen that your prayer is going to be part of a set of causes that makes it happen. So you'd better get on with it, as you and your prayer are part of God's overall purpose for the situation in which he is going to work. [12]

This is a pretty wild thought, no? God has ordained our prayer to be part of His plan of redemption in the world. This is both exciting and daunting. It raises the stakes for our prayer.

Cyprian would agree. We pray "Thy will be done," he wrote, so that "we should be able to do what God wishes." And, if we want to know what those wishes are, if we want to know what God's will is, we don't have to look far. God's will, according to Cyprian, is both what Jesus taught and what Jesus did. If you want to know the will of God, look at Jesus.[13]

This isn't about us trying harder to be better. It's about what *God is doing* in us as we pray. In, through, and after our prayer, God is inviting us to take part in His mission—our will is being conformed to the divine will. When we show forth charity, when we seek to bring healing, when we oppose injustice, when we give generously to the poor—we are doing God's will. When we love mercy and seek justice, we are being Christ's hands and feet.

We're all still learning to pray. We're novices at best, stumbling over our words, struggling to pay attention. We need to be taught, again and again, how to pray.

The good news is that prayer doesn't rely on your capability, but God's. "We do not know what to pray for as we ought," laments Paul in Romans 8. But "the Spirit himself intercedes for us with sighs too deep for words." We fumble around, struggling to name what we really want and need, but "the Spirit intercedes for the saints according to the will of God." We're not on our own—God not only hears our prayers; He gives them to us in the first place. God breathes our prayers in and through us.

And this brings us to the best news of all: God's capacity to hear is much greater than our inability to ask. We address a God who is "always more ready to hear than we to pray, and to give more than we either desire or deserve."

Maybe learning to pray is just learning to trust more and more that this is what God is like.

O God, the life of all who live, the light of the faithful, the strength of those who labor, and the repose of the dead: We thank you for the blessings of the day that is past, and humbly ask for your protection through the coming night. Bring us in safety to the morning hours; through him who died and rose again for us, your Son our Savior Jesus Christ. Amen.

Collect for Protection,
the *Book of Common Prayer*

5

Keeping Time
Living in Rhythms of Prayer

In western New York, autumn means cool, crisp mornings and beautiful fall leaves. Growing up there, autumn meant apple picking, tossing a football with my dad, backpacking trips, the smell of campfires, hot cider. Autumn is a season of bright, warm sights, scents, and flavors, all building anticipation for what comes in December: Christmas (and my birthday).

In Texas, autumn feels more than slightly different. We mark the beginning of fall not with the start of school, when temperatures persist in the triple digits, and not by the first crisp morning, which might not occur until November. Instead, we know fall has begun when pumpkin spice lattes appear in shops. We sweat our way to Halloween, pretending it's fall when we're really still stuck in a long epilogue to summer.

Like many other ways of marking time, the pumpkin spice latte is all about our consumption. Our seasons are defined and driven by consumerism. This year Halloween decorations went on sale in late July—the earliest start to "pumpkintide" I've encountered yet.

Advertisements, entertainment, and social media encourage us to get excited and get out our wallets to mark the next Big Season.

We might well question all this seasonal consumerism. But the marketing works because it taps into a deep desire: to mark together the passing of time. We want milestones and we want to share them. In that sense, it's understandable we want to enjoy an autumnal latte with a friend.

MARKING TIME

We crave seasonal markers because we were made to live in rhythms. If the natural world is ordered by seasons, so is our social and cultural life. For a good part of our lives, the most definitive structure comes from education. We start a new grade; take holiday, winter, and summer breaks; celebrate graduations; and do it all over again. Leaving this cycle behind might explain post-college disorientation—until then, the school year is the primary organization of time we've known.

In other eras of history (and other places in the world today), years were defined by seasons of plowing, planting, and harvesting. We're odd in being so disconnected from these rhythms. Our schedules change to a new "season"—an interesting word choice—of a television series or sports league instead of the gathering of a crop or harvesting of wild game.

The ways we mark time do more than add a gloss to our lives. Calendars shape our expectations, they invite our attention, they make claims about what is most significant. They aren't neutral, in other words. National holidays, for example, aim at deepening civic and patriotic bonds. They put before us a vision of what is good—what means the most.

This seems to be growing increasingly obvious in recent years. Consider, for example, replacing Columbus Day with Indigenous

People Day. Or the growth of "awareness" and "heritage months," including Black history month since 1976, women's history month since 1987, and LGBTQ pride month since 1999. These designated months are enshrined in our political and educational institutions, and not without controversy.

But changing the calendar isn't a new thing. During the French Revolution, as anti-Christian fervor reached a pitch, radicals instituted a new calendar that declared the beginning of the republic as "Year One." To purge Catholicism from France, revolutionaries needed to secularize the calendar itself. (It's worth comparing this to recent calls to abandon the dating system of BC, or "before Christ," and AD, "anno domini" or "in the year of our Lord," for the more secular BCE and CE, "before common era" and "common era.")

Each of these controversies proves my point: How we mark time matters. Our organization of the year shapes our collective memory, which in turn shapes our identity. Little wonder, then, that the early church, a tenuous religious minority in a pagan empire, was keenly interested in creating its own calendar.

So how did the church mark time?

And what does any of this have to do with prayer?

LIVING IN TIME, INHABITING ETERNITY

We experience time as one thing after another. Time, we think, is something finite, something that passes. This way of experiencing time is what the Orthodox theologian Alexander Schmemann calls *chronos*. In *For the Life of the World*, Schmemann writes that *chronos* is *quantitative* time: It's something we measure and count, something we keep or spend or waste. It's a resource we try to control through endless busyness, time-saving tricks, and anti-aging treatments. We know we're living in *chronos* when everything we do aims at extracting maximal experience, fulfillment, and productivity from time.

It often seems that *chronos* is all there is to time. Time only has meaning that we impose on it—the start of a new school year, our favorite sport season, or the holidays that offer a break from the cycle of productivity. As we grow older, we weary of these impositions of meaning. Life is just one darn thing after another, to paraphrase Mark Twain. That's *chronos* in a nutshell.

But we're meant to inhabit another dimension of time: what Schmemann calls *kairos*. *Kairos* is God's time; it is "the time of liturgical celebration," as he puts it. It is *qualitative* time. It is, simply, eternity.

> **In Christ, God's time has broken into our time. Eternity has entered into history. *Kairos* has invaded *chronos*.**

How do *chronos* and *kairos* relate? Schmemann says, "It seems to me that eternity might not be the stopping of time, but precisely its resurrection and gathering. The fragmentation of time, its division, is the fall of eternity. [We] thirst for the transformation of time into what it should be—the receptacle, the chalice of eternity."[1]

In Christ, God's time has broken into our time. Eternity has entered into history. *Kairos* has invaded *chronos*. This means that every time we reenact Christ's resurrection, every time we celebrate the liturgy, we participate in the transformation of time.

That's why Schmemann calls us to inhabit "liturgical time." Liturgical time, we might say, is *chronos* filled to the brim with *kairos*. Or, as Episcopalian priest Porter C. Taylor puts it, "Liturgical time is not the cessation of time; this could not be further from the truth. Liturgical time is in fact the thickening and deepening of time, it is time made more real; no, it is time made most real."[2]

This explains what early Christians did with the calendar. Early Christians understood that the risen Christ changed everything—even time itself must be reconceived in light of the resurrection. So they went about doing it. They reordered the week around the day of Christ's triumph, the new Sabbath. They structured their year around Easter, the great feast everything else pointed forward or backward to. Each week, and each year, was structured by a rhythm of commemorations, feasts, and fasts. And all of this ordering of yearly, weekly, and daily time helped Christians inhabit eternity. What did this look like?

PRAYER AND THE CHRISTIAN YEAR: LEARNING THE CHURCH CALENDAR

Jews had been observing holy days for centuries, but the first Christians did not have their own calendar. By the middle of the second century, the feast of Pascha emerged, when Christians marked Christ's suffering, death, and rising from the dead. Christians celebrated this festival annually (around the time of the Jewish Passover) after a season of preparatory fasting. Controversies over when to start the feast were addressed by the Council of Nicaea in 325, which ruled that Easter should begin on the Sunday after the first full moon after the spring equinox.[3]

By that time, other holy days, including commemorations of martyrs, had populated the Christian calendar. The Feast of the Nativity, or Christmas, was celebrated on a date calculated from Christ's conception (many held that Mary conceived Jesus on March 25).[4] We don't know exactly when Advent emerged, but by the 400s there was a well-established season of penitence and fasting in preparation for Christ's birth. These and other festivals and holy days made up a calendar that would be honed over the centuries and would end up dramatically shaping Western civilization.[5]

This calendar invites us into a rhythm of seasons, to relive the great story of sacred history. Or, you might say, when we follow the calendar, we reenact the drama.[6]

Advent: A season of expectant waiting when we reenact the prayerful waiting of God's people who are longing and preparing for Christ to come.

Christmas: A season of celebrating the incarnation, the mystery of God made man. We reenact the wonder of people coming to Bethlehem to adore the King.

Epiphany: We reenact and bear witness to Christ's revealing God to all people.

Lent (culminating in Holy Week): A season of repentance, of following Christ to the cross. We reenact His forty days of fasting and prayer in the desert. In Holy Week we reenact the confused disciples, who follow (and fail to follow) Christ through His suffering, trial, and death.

Easter (and Ascension): We reenact the shock of finding an empty tomb, and the joy of being greeted by our risen Lord. It's a season of celebrating our resurrected life, Christ's triumph over sin and death.

Pentecost: We reenact the founding of the church by the sending of the Holy Spirit.

Ordinary Time: We reenact the mission of the early church, empowered by the Spirit to fulfill the Great Commission. It is a season of growth, of going deeper into the sacred mystery of God's love.

What is this all about? What's the point? To walk alongside Jesus. We follow our Lord from His first days growing in Mary's womb, to His birth, through His ministry, into His holy passion and death, to the triumph of His resurrection and His ascension to the Father, and finally, to the sending of the Holy Spirit at Pentecost.

One of the things I've found most helpful about the liturgical calendar is the way it focuses my attention in prayer. It's simply not possible to focus on everything equally and all at once. The church's calendar centers our gaze on one facet of the whole. One way to get started is to pray through the calendar. Every day, pray and reflect on the collect for the week from the *Book of Common Prayer*. These collects invite us into the meaning of each liturgical season.

So during Lent, our prayers focus on repentance. We take a long, sustained look at our lives, pray for the grace to see where we've gone wrong, and, with God's help, repent—change direction. And during the great celebration of Eastertide, we turn our eyes to the victory won by Christ. Sin and death have been defeated! This good news merits a joyful feast—fifty days of feasting, to be precise. Easter is longer than Lent, because Christ's victory is so much greater than our sin.

And Easter is not only the climax of the Christian year, but also what defines the Christian week.

PRAYER AND THE CHRISTIAN WEEK: CREATED TO GIVE THANKS

Have you ever wondered what early Christian worship was like? One of the best depictions comes from a text rediscovered only 150 years ago: the *Didache* (also known as *The Lord's Teaching Through the Twelve Apostles to the Nations*). The *Didache* is a catechetical work, likely from the first century—written within a generation of the apostles. Some church fathers thought it should be included in the canon; Clement of Alexandria quoted it as Scripture, and Irenaeus, Origen, Justin Martyr, and Cyprian all knew it well. And after being lost for centuries, a complete manuscript was discovered in the 1870s. Since then, we've had a window into what the early church taught those entering the faith. One of the topics? The rhythm of the Christian week.

From its beginnings, the church considered Sunday the Lord's Day. Sunday was the day of resurrection, the new Sabbath, a window into eternity. On Sunday, the church gathered to celebrate Christ's triumph over death and sin. Ignatius of Antioch, martyred in the early 100s, praised Sunday as the day "our Life arose."[7] And at the center of this celebration, at the pinnacle of the week, was Holy Communion. As the *Didache* instructs, "Every Lord's day gather yourselves together, and break bread, and give thanksgiving after having confessed your transgressions, that your sacrifice may be pure."[8]

Perhaps our Communion services are sometimes too somber. We focus on our sin and unworthiness, and recount the awful and bloody sacrifice required to save us. Of course, this is correct. We need to remember and confess our sin, and humility and reverence are fitting. But a funereal mood might obscure that Holy Communion is a celebration. It's quite literally a thanksgiving service (the Greek *eucharistia* means "thanksgiving"). It's a feast!

> Thanksgiving is what we were made for. To offer up what we've received is our purpose.

Holy Communion is the feast that structures the rest of the Christian week. It's not a break from ordinary life but rather the transformation of life. Here's how Schmemann puts it: "Eucharist—thanksgiving and praise—is the very form and content of the new life that God granted us when in Christ He reconciled us with Himself."[9] What we do on Sunday morning changes everything about the other six days.

These prayers of thanksgiving aren't a means to some other end. We don't pray them so that we'll feel more grateful, or be more "centered." Thanksgiving is, in fact, what we were made for. To offer up what we've received is, in fact, our purpose. It's what we'll do for eternity.

WEEKLY RHYTHM TODAY

For the early church, the week had a rhythm. How might we live into something similar? With lives structured much more by work and "time off," how can we learn to inhabit a different rhythm?

One easy way to begin is praying the Collect of the Day (found on pages 22–24 of the 2019 edition of the *Book of Common Prayer*). These prayers offer a weekly structure that prepares us for the Lord's Day.

Consider a small weekly fast—perhaps going without lunch on Friday, for example. During the time you'd normally spend cooking and eating, engage in a prayer practice that helps you focus on your hunger for God.

Designate Sundays as a day for gratitude. How might your community keep the feast? A simple, slow meal together framed by prayers of gratitude? A hymn-sing? Each of you bringing a "thing you love" to share about?

THE CHRISTIAN DAY: EVENING, AND MORNING, AND AT NOON, WILL I PRAY

Like the year and the week, the day was also structured by prayer. Christians picked up what faithful Jews had done for centuries, praying at morning light, after noontime, and at or after dusk. The pattern came from the Hebrew Scriptures. In Psalm 55:17, David declares, "Evening and morning and at noon I utter my complaint and moan, and he will hear my voice." And the prophet Daniel "got down upon his knees three times a day and prayed and gave thanks before his God" (Dan. 6:10).

Likewise, the *Didache* instructs new Christians, "pray this [the Lord's Prayer] three times a day."[10] In his treatise on prayer, Tertullian also encouraged Christians to pray at certain hours of the day. For Tertullian, as well as Origen and Clement of Alexandria, Christians ought to pray five times a day: morning and evening prayer, as well as the third (9:00 a.m.), sixth (noon), and ninth (3:00 p.m.) hours.

But what about Paul's instructions to the church in Thessalonica to "pray without ceasing" (1 Thess. 5:17 ESV)? How could anyone do this without neglecting work entirely? The church found an answer in Psalm 119:164. "Seven times a day I praise you for your righteous rules" (ESV). Hippolytus, a third-century martyr and bishop, instructed believers to follow the psalmist's example, praying "on rising, at the lighting of the evening lamp, at bedtime, at midnight" and "the third, sixth, and ninth hours of the day, being hours associated with Christ's Passion."[11]

> We join our voices to a chorus, harmonizing with medieval monks, early Christians huddled in the catacombs, and the prophets and psalmists before them.

This pattern would be formalized in the early sixth century by Benedict. In his Rule, Benedict established the canonical hours—the pattern that has defined Western monasticism to this day. Monks stop whatever they are doing (including sleeping) to pray at seven hours: matins and lauds (typically combined into one hour in the middle of the night), prime (dawn), terce (9:00 a.m.), sext (noon), none (3:00 p.m.), vespers (dusk), and compline (bedtime). Simply put, monks pray around the clock.

What about the rest of the church? Most Christians don't become monks. This is why the English reformer Thomas Cranmer sought to translate the monastic ideal into something ordinary Christians might practice: Morning and Evening Prayer. When we pray the Daily Office, we join our voices to a chorus, harmonizing with medieval monks, early Christians huddled in the catacombs, and the prophets and psalmists before them.

Another daily structure of prayer worth considering is the Examen. Outlined by Ignatius of Loyola, the Examen invites us to prayerfully attend to God's presence in our day. For those who joined the Jesuits, the order founded by Ignatius, the Examen was prayed twice a day—at noon and at day's end.

Self-examination isn't unique to Ignatian spirituality. Many Christian traditions have their own version: from Anglican, Puritan, and Methodist guides to examining one's conscience, to evangelical practices of personal examination. You could read Jonathan Edwards,[12] or John Wesley,[13] or Richard Foster[14] and find good help in the work of examining yourself.

Around the world, Christians across different denominations pray the Examen. It offers the daily opportunity to look backward and forward.

The Examen asks you to prayerfully reflect on when in the day you felt yourself drawing closer to God (your consolations) and moving away from God (your desolations). There are many variations on this form of prayerful reflection. It can take as little as five to fifteen minutes, and can be prayed at any time of day that works for you—perhaps first thing in the morning or at bedtime.

Here's a simple version of the five-step Examen:

1. Thank God for all that is good.
2. Ask for insight and light.
3. Look at yourself—what you did, felt, thought.
4. Offer the good to the Lord, and ask His forgiveness for the not good.
5. Offer to God what you'll do tomorrow.[15]

Whether the Daily Office, the Examen, or another practice entirely, our days are meant to be framed by conversation with God. For the Christian who wants to inhabit eternity, prayer is the best beginning and end to any day.

Practicing Life Together

We were made to live in rhythm. The rhythm of the year, the week, and the day gives structure, purpose, and meaning to everything we do. But time passes more quickly than we realize. As Annie Dillard puts it, "How we spend our days is, of course, how we spend our lives. What we do with this hour, and that one, is what we are doing."[16] Dillard is right. Yet many of us feel somewhat helpless about our spending. Our days seem dictated for us, bound by commitments, rituals, and seasons imposed by the broader culture. Before we know it, our life is already structured for us, and all our time accounted for.

We can learn to live by another rhythm. Our hours and days can be formed, and transformed, by the ebb and flow of liturgical time. From its beginnings, the church has cared about the shape and structure of time, given attention to the shape of the year, the week, the day. What difference might it make to follow this structure?

How might living by the church's calendar change your experience of time?

How might habits of prayer, lived out day by day and week by week, make up a life?

And how might we live it out in community?

Almighty God, you have given us grace at this time, with one accord to make our common supplications to you; and you have promised through your well-beloved Son that when two or three are gathered together in his Name you will grant their requests: Fulfill now, O Lord, our desires and petitions as may be best for us; granting us in this world knowledge of your truth, and in the age to come life everlasting. Amen.

A Prayer of St. John Chrysostom,
the *Book of Common Prayer*

6

Practicing Common Prayer

"What is the secret of Christian community?" I asked my great-aunt Bernadine years ago, as an earnest twenty-three-year-old. Both Paige and I were quite interested in her answer. At the time, we lived in the community house I described in chapter 2. We hoped, one day, to be part of leading an intentional Christian community.

I asked my aunt because she was a Catholic nun, a School Sister of Notre Dame. For decades, Aunt Bernadine lived with her vowed sisters, serving and teaching in Chile, Puerto Rico, and Connecticut. Her extended family had gathered to celebrate her sixtieth jubilee, giving me an opportunity to ask my question. I eagerly waited for her to share some key she'd discovered over decades of life in community.

My aunt's reply was quick and to the point: "Well, we eat together and we pray together. That's what makes our community." I remember being disappointed. I had hoped for something more sophisticated—some deep insight or brilliant quote. This answer seemed rather basic.

Community is a buzzword. It serves as a catchall for our hopes and aspirations to belong. It's innocuous—nobody is against community in principle—and that makes it ubiquitous. There's a significant publishing industry on the topic—each new bestseller promises to unlock genuine community.

But Aunt Bernadine didn't offer a secret. She simply stated the obvious: Her community was founded on common goods—praying and eating with each other. Over time I've realized that her answer was not at all disappointing. Rather, she named a truth about community that is blessedly simple and deeply profound.

Corporate prayer and shared meals invite us into communion—a word not incidentally related to "community." When we gather around the table, face to face, shoulder to shoulder, we share in the life-giving bounty of God's good creation. When we pray together, we commune with God and with each other. We come to know and be known by each other; we bear each other's burdens.

"Eat together and pray together" might sound basic, but it certainly isn't easy. It's probably easier if you've vowed to do these things, just as my great-aunt did as a twenty-year-old. But this way of living shouldn't be reserved only for the vowed religious. It is possible to structure our lives so that corporate prayer and shared meals are built in to our days and weeks.

And, by the way, if you find yourself in the post-college years lacking close friends, the best way to find them might be by inviting others into these practices. Eating and praying together is a great way to cultivate friendship. Making community takes effort, but it isn't complicated. It's as simple as committing to pray and eat together.

How do we do this? We've already discussed shared meals. What practices of prayer, in particular, can a community commit to?

MONASTICISM FOR THE REST OF US: CRANMER'S BOOK

Thomas Cranmer would have liked my aunt's answer. The good archbishop, who guided the Church of England through the tumultuous years of the English Reformation, believed that praying together mattered immensely. After Henry VIII broke from Rome in the 1530s and questions swirled about reforming the church, Cranmer's attention centered on this question: How might the Church of England cultivate true godliness?

Cranmer believed that spiritual renewal would only come about if ordinary Christians were steeped in Scripture and in prayer. All of his reforms sought this goal. First, the prayers and reading of Scripture must be in English. Second, the lectionary, or assigned readings from the Bible, must walk the church through the story of sacred Scripture in a cohesive way. And third, the local church must be a place where all Christians might come, morning and evening, to pray.

Cranmer believed that the life of prayer isn't just for priests or monks. By translating the monastic and cathedral prayers into the Daily Office (Morning and Evening Prayer) Cranmer was inviting every Christian to be a kind of monk.

For nearly five centuries, Cranmer's *Book of Common Prayer* has been a gift to the whole church. While Anglicans (and Episcopalians) are the most likely to use the *BCP*, Christians from across denominations and traditions find it useful in their prayer lives. I personally know Baptists, Presbyterians, and Methodists who regularly pray with the *BCP* and find it a rich resource.

Of course, the *BCP* isn't your only option for communal prayer. From Phyllis Tickle's *Divine Hours* series, to the Presbyterian *Book of Common Worship Daily Prayer*, you might prefer another, depending on your tradition. Of the many editions of the *Book of Common Prayer*, I recommend trying the 2019 edition, published by the Anglican Church in North America, the denomination I belong to. It's user-friendly and clear.

The *BCP* does two things particularly well—you might say it offers two gifts to the church.

THE COLLECT: CARING FOR WORDS

In the tradition I grew up in, we were nervous about written prayers. We thought they were "rote," making prayer into a mechanical recitation rather than something that arose from the heart. Far better to pray spontaneously, using your own words.

But does spontaneity always mean more?

In other areas of life, spontaneous words aren't necessarily better. Think of a lover who wants to express devotion to his beloved. Which is more significant: to make something up on the spot, or to craft a thoughtful letter or pretty piece of poetry? Both! Each has its place, and each can be meaningful.

What about at a funeral? Would it be more "authentic" for someone to ad-lib a eulogy for their beloved spouse or parent, or take the time to choose each word carefully?

During a wedding, would it be inauthentic for the couple to borrow their promises? To vow to "have and to hold from this day forward, for better for worse, for richer for poorer, in sickness and in health . . ."? (Lines that come from the *Book of Common Prayer*, by the way.)

When it comes to the words that matter most—wedding vows, eulogies, retirement toasts, love letters—it can be just as genuine to use words that have been thoughtfully crafted. Whether we author them ourselves, or borrow from another, written words reflect *care*.

And this brings us back to the *Book of Common Prayer*. One of its gifts is a careful attention to grammar—its care for words. Cranmer's book is premised on the idea that prayer involves learning a language. As my friend Nicholas puts it, the *BCP* understands that the words we use in prayer are not merely expressive. They're *formative*. Our words don't merely give voice to something we already know and experience. They shape us; they form what we understand. "You can only act in the world you can *see*," writes theologian

Stanley Hauerwas, "but you can only *see* by learning to *say*" (emphasis added).[1]

One way the *BCP* cares for words is in its "collects." These prayers *collect* the people of God—they gather our thoughts and focus our attention as we begin to worship.

Every aspect of a collect is intentional—each word choice, the ordering of each phrase. Most collects follow the same structure: a preamble, a petition, and a conclusion.

First, in the preamble, we address God, and highlight one aspect of God's character. What about God—and what God has done—grounds our request? What aspect of God's character gives us confidence to make the petition that will follow? After all, our prayer does not hinge on our ability, but on who God is. We begin by remembering something true about God.

Consider the opening of the Collect for the Sixth Sunday of Easter: "O God, you have prepared for those who love you such good things as surpass our understanding." Here, toward the end of Eastertide, we remember that Christ promised to prepare us a home where we will eternally dwell with Him. We remember that our destiny is beatitude, blessedness, being with God forever.

Consider taking ten minutes, right now, to slowly pray the Collect for the Sixth Sunday of Easter:

> O God, you have prepared for those who love you such good things as surpass our understanding: Pour into our hearts such love toward you, that we, loving you in all things and above all things, may obtain your promises, which exceed all that we can desire; through Jesus Christ our Lord, who lives and reigns with you and the Holy Spirit, one God, forever and ever. Amen.

In its second part, a collect voices our request. It asks something. Having named God's great plans for those who love Him, we want to love Him more: "Pour into our hearts such love . . ." What a great thing to ask: Give us more love. We want to love more, and for all of our loves to be rightly ordered toward love of God.

Sometimes, the petition includes a "so that" clause. We ask for something, and then we say why we're asking it—what we're hoping for. In this case, we hope to "obtain your promises, which exceed all that we can desire." This collect returns to what we named in the address: God has promised more than we can imagine and, because we want that, we ask Him to pour love into our hearts.

Finally, in its third part, a collect articulates why we are able to ask this. Thus, the Easter Six collect concludes, "Through Jesus Christ our Lord, who lives and reigns with you and the Holy Spirit, one God, for ever and ever." We invoke our Mediator, Jesus Christ, in whose name we pray. Because we are united to Christ, and filled with the Holy Spirit, we can petition God our Father.

Understanding these parts of the collects helps us see the richness packed into these short prayers. We learn who God is; we recognize our needs and our hopes; we ask for something we might not otherwise think of, but that we deeply long for.

Collects, like poetry, reward careful, slow, repeated reading. You could ponder, and pray, this collect for days and not exhaust its meaning. And the *BCP* offers over a hundred of these carefully formed, theologically rich prayers. What a gift.

LEARNING TO LISTEN: MORNING AND EVENING PRAYER

If collects are one gift of the *Book of Common Prayer*, another is the context in which we often say them. The heart of common prayer is the Daily Office: Morning and Evening Prayer, as well as Compline. (Evening Prayer is typically said around dinnertime, while saying Compline is the last thing you do before bed.)

It's hard to sum up all the richness of the Daily Office, but let me highlight four things: These prayers help us listen to God, they frame our day around prayer, they join us together, and they unite us to the church around the world.

First, the Daily Office gets us listening. The *Book of Common Prayer* has been described as "Scripture organized for worship." Most of the words in the *BCP* are from the Bible—perhaps as much as 85 percent. Praying with the *BCP* doesn't replace reading the Bible—in fact, it encourages it. When we pray the Daily Office we work through the Psalms, the prayer book of God's people, and the story of Scripture, through the assigned lectionary readings. When we pray Morning and Evening Prayer, we are praying Scripture.

Our prayer is always a response to God. God initiates prayer; we only speak to God because He has first spoken to us. It is fitting, then, for our prayer to begin with listening. We hear Scripture in the readings, we pray Scripture in the canticles and collects, and then we add our own voices in additional requests and thanksgiving.

Second, the Daily Office organizes our day around prayer. The offices give us prayers for every part of the day, turning our day-to-day life into an ongoing conversation with God. In this way they help us better inhabit the rhythms of time. See, for example, the Collect for the Renewal of Life, prayed on Monday mornings:

> O God, the King eternal, whose light divides the day from the night and turns the shadow of death into the morning: Drive far from us all wrong desires, incline our hearts to keep your law, and guide our feet into the way of peace; that, having done your will with cheerfulness during the day, we may, when night comes, rejoice to give you thanks.

This prayer reminds us that every morning is a gift from our King. We ask Him to direct us throughout the day, anticipating our gratitude for His guidance at day's end. When we get there, we'll close our day with words like these from the Collect for Protection, prayed every Wednesday evening:

> O God, the life of all who live, the light of the faithful, the strength of those who labor, and the repose of the dead: We thank you for the blessings of the day that is past, and humbly ask for your protection through the coming night. Bring us in safety to the morning hours; through him who died and rose again for us, your Son our Savior Jesus Christ.

As Alan Jacobs notes, this prayer would have been taken quite seriously. In early modern England, darkness brought all sorts of spiritual and physical dangers. Threats real and imagined caused no little amount of anxiety over the coming of nighttime in Cranmer's world.[2]

The night may not seem so dangerous to us. But it may still hold fatigue, anxiety, insomnia, the stress of what tomorrow brings—a tomorrow that we're not promised, but that by God's mercy we may welcome with the morning light. At day's end, we still need to ask for God's protection.

Third, the Daily Office joins us together. For a decade, Paige and I have been part of a small community that prays the Morning Office together. When you pray the Daily Office with others, it's like walking a familiar hiking trail. Side by side, you come to know your fellow pilgrims' ups and downs, heartaches and hopes.

Every morning, the office includes time for "intercessions and thanksgivings." Brazos Fellows have prayed for one another's parents battling cancer, for difficult job searches, for big decisions. We've prayed for pregnancies and about miscarriages. We've lifted up each other's loneliness and chronic illness and anxiety. We've prayed for family members and friends who've walked away from the faith.

We've celebrated when God answered prayers in ways we hoped; we've sat in silent grief after great loss. Praying the Daily Office turns a group into a people—a people who know and are known through prayer.

Fourth, the Daily Office unites us with the church. One of my favorite prayers from the *BCP* comes during Compline:

> Right now, at various places all across the planet, Christians are praying these offices. Christ's body prays without ceasing, across languages, national boundaries, and time zones.

Keep watch, dear Lord, with those who work, or watch, or weep this night, and give your angels charge over those who sleep. Tend the sick, Lord Christ; give rest to the weary, bless the dying, soothe the suffering, pity the afflicted, shield the joyous; and all for your love's sake. Amen.

At the close of day, we remember all God's children who come to this night in various states of grief, joy, suffering, fatigue, restlessness. We offer up the breadth of human experience to a God who hears and cares. This also means the church has prayed for *you*: If, at the end of a day, you found yourself joyful, busy, grieving, anxious, suffering, or just plain old weary, the church prayed this prayer for you.

And this is my favorite thing about the Daily Office. Right now, at various places all across the planet, Christians are praying these offices. At this very moment, a faithful believer is saying morning, or midday, or evening prayer.

Perhaps, even as you read these words, an aged couple is praying the Morning Office, lifting up wrinkled hands as they say the Te Deum; far from them, as evening grows near, a lonely student is putting down his books to find solace in the Magnificat; elsewhere, in Australia or Nigeria or British Columbia, some weary young mother whispers the words of Compline over her sleepy children. Christ's body prays without ceasing, across languages, national boundaries, and time zones.

When we pray the Daily Office, we add our voices to this unending chorus. And, even when we can't, the church is still praying with and for us.

SAYING NO: SOLITUDE AND SILENCE

As with the other practices in this book, there's a negation that goes hand in hand with common prayer. Saying yes to something usually involves saying no to other things. The person training for a marathon knows it's not enough to run lots of miles. There's also a long list of things (junk food, alcohol, late night parties) to renounce if they want to run their best.

While renouncing junk food or drunkenness seems obvious, the Christian life sometimes involves renouncing *good* things—at least for a season. Is this true of community? Is there a time and place for withdrawing from each other?

My friend Jess changed how I think about this question. In Christian circles, "community" is exalted—it is praised and encouraged ad naseum. Jess pointed out that this well-meant discourse "taught me that there is no place for loneliness. As a result, I did not learn how to be lonely. In other words, I did not recognize that loneliness can be just as edifying as rich friendship."

The desert fathers and mothers convinced Jess that being alone can have value. For ascetics like Anthony, and the many women and men who emulated his life, "isolation was not a burden to be endured, nor a reason for despair, but to take delight in their Abba Father."[3] These monastics followed Christ, who left behind both the crowd and His disciples to be alone (see Matt. 14:13; Luke 5:16). If Christ sought solitude for the sake of prayer, how much more do we need the same?

But most of us don't like to be alone. Stillness and silence are uncomfortable. But community and solitude need each other. In *Life Together*, Bonhoeffer writes, "The day together will be unfruitful without the day alone. . . . The mark of solitude is silence, just as speech is the mark of community. . . . One does not exist without the other."[4]

What might be the value of time spent alone? The value of practicing solitude and silence for an hour a week?

Where might you find a time and place to be still? To sit in silence and "know that I am God," as the psalmist exhorts us in Psalm 46:10?

And how might these times of intentional loneliness enrich times of togetherness? How might solitude and community require each other?

GETTING STARTED WITH COMMON PRAYER

At this point in the book, I hope that you and your friends are considering taking on a common rule—and committing to pray together. Great! Now what? How do you start?

The best advice I can give is to make some version of the Daily Office central to your community's rule. The Daily Office invites you into the church's prayers, while also providing a framework for your personal practice of prayer. Praying the Daily Office with others structures your common life around relationship with God.

So how do you get started with the Daily Office? What are the various things you should think through as you begin?[5]

What and when will you pray together? Unless you live in a communal house, it's probably too much to pray both the morning and evening offices together. Focus primarily on one. For example, the Brazos Fellows gather for Morning Prayer at 7:15 a.m. each weekday, Monday through Friday. Most days they pray Evening Prayer or Compline in their own homes. When we're all together for our weekly dinner, we'll conclude with one of the evening offices. If your work commitments make it impossible to meet daily, something is better than nothing—pray together a few times a week, and on your own the rest of the time.

What's included in the daily office? It takes about thirty minutes, start to finish, to pray the Morning or Evening Office. The Brazos Fellows pray with the 2019 *BCP*, including the full Bible readings assigned in the Daily Office lectionary. Toward the end, we take advantage of the opportunity to offer additional prayers. Then we sing the "hymn of the week" before concluding.

Where will you meet for prayer? Think about finding two alternating places to meet. The Brazos Fellows meet in a living room three mornings and at church the other two. Praying in someone's home provides a sense of warm welcome, it's easier for families and young kids to participate, and we enjoy tea or coffee while we pray. Praying in the church, on the other hand, helps us learn to belong and participate in a sacred space.

How will you get started? Who will lead? If you're new to the Daily Office, it might be helpful to do a bit of reading on how to lead the Office.[6] If you know someone who is familiar with the *BCP*, ask them to lead your community through an "instructed Morning Prayer" that teaches you how to use the Prayer Book and where to find the Psalms and readings. Leading others in the Daily Office is a great way to enter more deeply into the prayers, so we encourage every member of our community to take turns officiating. Serve as the officiant for a full week so you grow more comfortable and familiar with leading.

What challenges might you run into? Sometimes people arrive late. Sometimes, in a difficult season, a member struggles to attend regularly. To respect everyone's commitments, it's best to start punctually.

Those who arrive later can slip in and join as they can. We all need grace: whether for being a bit late, struggling to lead smoothly, or mispronouncing an obscure Old Testament name. We extend each other grace while holding one another accountable to the practices we've committed to.

Of course, you'll need to adapt these practices to your own context. Your community might choose to begin earlier or later in the morning. Perhaps it makes more sense to say Evening Prayer together. Perhaps you will opt not to include a hymn, or perhaps your group will decide to chant the psalms. You might decide to include only one of the two assigned readings from the lectionary. Adapt how and when you pray together to your particular situation.

About a decade after talking with my great-aunt Bernadine, the first cohort of Brazos Fellows started their work of study, prayer, and discernment. But it took me a few years to realize how much our community was based on the "secret" she told me. Our common rule is centered around weekly meals and daily prayer. The two retreats we go on also follow that pattern: Our fall retreat focuses on prayer and our spring retreat on the spirituality of food. Now, when I find myself talking to someone about the fellowship, and they ask what we do, I echo Aunt Bernadine: "Well, we eat together, and we pray together."

Study: Learning to Wonder

PART THREE

Loving the Lord with All Our Mind: The Life of Study
Our Inheritance: Receiving the Gift of Tradition
Practicing Reading Together

O God, the light of the minds that know you, the life of the souls that love you, and the strength of the wills that serve you: Help us so to know you that we may truly love you, and so to love you that we may fully serve you, whom to serve is perfect freedom; through Jesus Christ our Lord. Amen.

A Prayer for Knowing and Loving God,
the *Book of Common Prayer*

7

Loving the Lord with All Our Mind
The Life of Study

In 1959, during the tense days of the Cold War, Walter M. Miller Jr. published *A Canticle for Leibowitz*. The novel is set in a Catholic monastery in the post-apocalyptic American Southwest. After a nuclear holocaust destroys society as we know it, a fictional order of monks maintains knowledge over a thousand years. Winner of the 1961 Hugo Award, the book is a gripping and philosophically fascinating read.

A Canticle for Leibowitz projects into a fictional future something quite real in the church's past. For significant periods of the church's history, monastics and monasteries have been the custodians of knowledge. Monks preserved and expanded scholarship and literature throughout the Middle Ages, and many ancient classics, from Virgil to Cicero to Aristotle, survive today because they were carefully kept and copied in monasteries.

It's difficult to overstate the importance of medieval monks in preserving and advancing learning. To name only a few: Paula of Rome (AD 347–404), a widow-turned-monastic who helped edit and publish Jerome's Latin translation of the Bible; the scholar and monk Cassiodorus (AD 485–585), who taught monks to read, understand, and copy literature (both sacred and secular); Patriarch Timothy I (AD 728–823) who, along with other Syrian monastics, translated Aristotle, the Bible, writings of the church fathers, and saints' lives, preserving these works for generations of Arabic-speaking Christians.[1] Many more could be named.

In a time that often holds a low view both of the so-called Dark Ages and of vowed religious life, this might be the only legacy of medieval monasticism we appreciate. At least those monks kept Virgil around for us!

Our own day idealizes, if not idolizes, learning. We prize degrees, celebrating graduations more than we would baptisms. Knowledge is not only a chief good but a right—we demand to be able to know.

At the same time, education is in crisis. Culture warriors fight over public school curriculum, the cost of college balloons even as enrollment drops, and the study of humanities continues its steep decline, all while politicians and pundits debate over how to stay ahead of global rivals. We don't agree on what education is, how it should be done, and what it aims at.

Interestingly, the Christian tradition is somewhat ambiguous about knowledge and learning. On the one hand, God gave us rational minds, and Scripture calls us to use them. Study—especially the study of sacred Scripture—is central to the Christian life. What's more, the apostles, and many saints since, deeply engaged with pagan learning—thus Cassiodorus and Timothy I.

On the other hand, there are plenty of scriptural warnings about knowledge. Things went wrong when Adam and Eve grasped after knowledge forbidden to them. Christ warns of following "the tradition of men" (Mark 7:8); Paul writes that "God chose what is foolish in the world to shame the wise" (1 Cor. 1:27). No wonder Tertullian proclaimed, "What has Athens to do with Jerusalem?" (In other words, pagan learning and philosophy have nothing to do with the truth about God.)

How do we understand this ambiguity? When is knowing good, when not so good?

How should we think of learning and education? Of what value are they?

In what sense are Christians called to the life of the mind? And what should this look like?

THE PROBLEM WITH CURIOSITY

In the modern West, we celebrate curiosity. You'd be hard-pressed to find a children's book, marketing campaign, or educational institution that doesn't laud being curious. But not so the Christian tradition. I remember my surprise when I learned, from a Paul Griffiths essay, about the traditional Christian distinction between the vice of curiosity and the virtue of studiousness.

Curiositas, in the classical sense, is not exactly what we mean by "curiosity" today. Classically, the curious one aims at possessing knowledge to use for his own benefit; in contrast, the studious one recognizes that "anything that can be known by any one of us is already known to God and has been given to us as unmerited gift."[2]

> In its classical meaning, curiosity seeks to master; study seeks with humility and gratitude.

Drawing on Augustine, Griffiths parses the difference between these modes of learning: Curiosity seeks to possess, to master; study seeks with humility and gratitude. Curiosity is insatiable; study is attentive, even contemplative. Curiosity pursues knowledge to gain control; studiousness means learning out of delight. This difference explains the ambiguity of the Christian tradition toward knowledge—it explains why Adam and Eve's grasping after knowledge was wicked and why Paul knows pagan poetry well enough to recite it to his Stoic listeners in Athens.

Crucially, the difference between *curiositas* and studiousness is ontological—it is rooted in different understandings of reality itself. Griffiths explains that while the curious treat the world as something to be manipulated and controlled for one's own purposes, "the studious person inhabits a world of gifts."[3] If this world is not of our own making, but is freely given by God, then so is our knowledge. We only know to the extent that we participate, or share, in what God knows.

This understanding of knowledge runs contrary to so many modern assumptions. In fact, Griffiths points out, the academy today treats *curiositas* as if it were a virtue. We define knowledge as proprietary, we prize innovation, we leverage all our study toward the creation of a marketable "personal brand."

And studying at a Christian college or seminary does not immunize us against these temptations. As Augustine wrote in his *Confessions*, curiosity can even motivate the study of theology: "Even in religion itself the motive is seen when God is 'tempted' by demands for 'signs and wonders' desired not for any salvific end but only for the thrill."[4]

Reading Griffiths wrecked me. I was in graduate school, and after finishing all I could say was, "Oh no." With unnerving precision, Griffiths diagnosed me. I was tempted to approach my studies not for their own sake but for what this work could get me—the grade, the publication, the job. I was driven by the desire Griffiths named: to "be known as one who knows."[5]

EDUCATION AND THE POVERTY OF PROFESSIONALISM

While the main problem was inside my own heart, I was also lured into *curiositas* by the ways our society understands knowledge and learning. What is education for? To make us productive citizens. To maximize our earning potential. To prepare us for certain jobs. And, the higher you go in education, the more your degree(s) become markers of success, status, and belonging.

This approach is a far cry from the liberal arts tradition, a tradition inherited, adapted, and cultivated by the church. Classically, the point of being educated in the liberal arts was not to increase your status or wealth but to *liberate* you. The point is to help you live as *free*— despite your situation or circumstances, able to live the good life.

But we modern people tend to think of education not as something that opens up life but something we finish so as to get to the rest of life. Learning is a box you tick to finally get to the "real world," whatever that means.

Two things result from this utilitarian approach to learning. One is professionalism: Education, we think, prepares us to "be professionals." And what it means to "be a professional" is for one's identity to be wrapped up in one's work; the thing we do becomes who we think we are. That's why when we meet someone our first question is often, "What do you do?"

Second, if the intellectual life is just about preparing for particular professions, then it's not really for anyone else. You'd only go on studying if you want to be a professor, or a minister, or a lawyer. The rest of us have gone as far in our studies as was absolutely required, and now we'll leave those kinds of conversations and books, that intellectual work, to the professionals.

Little wonder, given these assumptions, that we read less and less every year. In 2020, Americans between the ages of fifteen and forty-four read "for personal interest" for an average of twelve minutes per day; the same demographic spent a daily average of two hours and eight minutes watching TV.[6] And in 2021, Americans who are book readers (83 percent of the population) reported reading less—on average, three fewer books a year than they reported reading annually between 2002–16.[7] If you read at least one book a month, you're in a rapidly shrinking minority.

> It's a terribly wrong idea to believe that serious reading and serious thinking is reserved only for some, or limited to one stage of life.

Of course, many social, cultural, and technological factors contribute to this decline in reading. But underneath these is a terribly wrong idea: that the intellectual life isn't for everybody. We believe that serious reading and serious thinking is reserved only for some, or limited to one stage of life.

But study *can* and *should* be a lifelong pursuit. Wrestling with big questions, wondering about the meaning of things, deliberating and debating and pursuing truth together—these are "hidden pleasures" of being human, as philosopher Zena Hitz puts it. The intellectual life is too *human* to reserve it only for academics.[8]

How might studiousness become a way of life?

And, more particularly, how might study be part of the Christian life?

WHY THEOLOGY IS FOR AMATEURS

"Why should I study more theology?" So asked one of our Brazos Fellows several years ago. She and I were discussing what she might do after the fellowship. Seminary was a consideration, but she wondered what would be the point, given that she wasn't interested in pursuing pastoral ministry. So...why bother? Why give several more years to theological education?

It's a fair question, and one that reminded me of similar statements I've heard over the years. Perhaps you've heard them too:

I'm not an academic—those deep questions are beyond me.

You'd better be sure of a job in your denomination before spending time and money on seminary.

Some people should study theology, but it's not for everyone.

These sentiments are usually sincere, and in some sense they're not wrong. Certainly not every Christian should enroll in seminary. But I think these statements also reveal several assumptions we should question.

Assumption #1: Theological study is only for the super smart people. We often speak of theology as an academic discipline—something you need advanced training to understand. Theological study is for folks who would gladly spend an afternoon debating an obscure point in Thomas Aquinas.

Assumption #2: Theological study is for professionals, a means to an end. It's not a good in itself but something you get through in order to gain credentials. Some jobs require a level of theological training. We *do* need theologically trained pastors and teachers. And most of the rest of us shouldn't go to seminary. Nonetheless, these assumptions constrain our imagination for what theological study is and who it's for.

To begin with, the studious life is not solely (or even primarily) for academics. We're all called to be students—to study God, to study ourselves, to study the world He created and sustains. As Griffiths puts it, "All study is a form of lovemaking, of work proper to amateurs rather than professionals."[9] By "amateur," Griffiths doesn't mean someone who is shoddy or unserious, but someone who does the thing out of love.

Perhaps amateur theology is just part of being Christian. How so? We are called to love God, and any good lover always wants to know more of the Beloved. We attend to what we love; we more deeply love that to which we attend. In other words, theologians in particular ought to be amateurs.

This kind of theological study can never be instrumentalized. Theology is not a means to some other end, no matter how good—getting a job, winning an argument, or "changing the world." Genuine theological study, to the extent that it involves seeking to know and love God, is a good *in and of itself*. Or, to put it another way, every Christian is called to some degree of theological study, because every Christian is called to love God with our minds.

That's why study is part of this common rule. You and your community are invited to become amateur theologians. What might this look like? The answer to that question should begin with a doctrine of being *creatures*.

STUDY AS GRATITUDE

We live every day with a mystery: the fact that we exist. We awaken into a world that is not of our own making, a world that we did nothing to bring about or earn. Our life comes to us as a gift, entirely undeserved, entirely from another. And the fitting response to this fact is gratitude.

Gratitude is proper to our creaturely existence; it is the first and most fundamental thing we owe by virtue of being creatures. "He who made me is good, and he is my good too," Augustine writes in his *Confessions*. "Rejoicing, I thank him for all those good gifts which made me what I was, even as a boy."[10]

Conversely, the Christian tradition warns of the danger of ingratitude. As Ignatius of Loyola warned, ingratitude is "the cause, beginning, and origin of all evils and sins."[11] There's really no sin that is not somehow rooted in a lack of gratitude for God's generosity in creating and providing for us. And the inevitable effect of ingratitude, like all sin, is unhappiness.

But the relation between happiness and gratitude is an interesting one. We tend to think of gratitude as a feeling, a sense of gladness or delight. That's true as far as it goes. But gratitude is more deliberate than that. It involves our memories and our attention. Put another way, gratitude is not merely an emotional experience but something we *intend*, something we *practice*.

How do we practice gratitude? With our attention. What we attend to, what we remember—what we study—either feeds or stifles gratitude. The way to repay a generous gift is to give it your attention. And we could say the inverse: To forget, to ignore, to tire of the gift, would be failures of gratitude.

This is why we can't leave gratitude up to chance—we can't just hope that we'll feel thankful. Instead, we must become students of the gift. If we want to deepen gratitude, we must cultivate wonder.

STUDY AS WONDER

What's the longest you've ever looked at an onion?

If your answer is more than a few seconds, I wager you've read *The Supper of the Lamb*. In one chapter, Robert Farrar Capon invites readers to spend an hour in the company of an onion. It sounds silly, but I couldn't recommend it more highly. Every year, the Brazos Fellows do this on our spring retreat—and love it. Capon wants you to see the remarkable thing that is a yellow onion, a thing that doesn't *have* to exist, but nonetheless does. Why? God "*likes* onions, therefore they are."[12]

It's precisely by attending to the small and mundane that we learn to be students of God's creation. Capon writes, "Man's real work is to look at the things of the world and to love them for what they are. That is, after all, what God does, and man was not made in God's image for nothing."[13] When a student attends to the world, he imitates God, who sustains His creation with loving attention.

But wondering doesn't always come easily. Without Capon's encouragement, I would've never wondered about an onion enough to take the time to peel away the pearlescent skin, separate each layer like a set of Russian *matryoshka* dolls, notice the substance and smell of the thing. It turns out an onion is beautiful and well worth the time—but only if you wonder.

We often name this kind of wondering "curiosity," but we now know that *curiositas* is a vice. So what makes one thing *curiositas* and another wonder?

Is it a matter only of inward disposition? Of motive? Or would the work of learning look noticeably different if you approached with wonder?

Griffiths says the curious person doesn't want to deeply and thoroughly explore something. They skim along the surface, happy with superficial understanding. The curious one craves novelty—their appetite for it is never sated.

Children are better at wonder: They encounter the world as a fresh surprise, a mystery begging to be solved, an invitation to ask and poke and pry. This is what drives a two-year-old to ask dad for a second, third, and even *fourth* reading of Eric Carle's *The Very Hungry Caterpillar*. (Can you tell I write from experience?)

G. K. Chesterton surmised that children are most like God precisely in their capacity for wonder. Here's how he put it:

> Because children have abounding vitality, because they are in spirit fierce and free, therefore they want things repeated and unchanged. They always say, "Do it again"; and the grown-up person does it again until he is nearly dead. For grown-up people are not strong enough to exult in monotony. But perhaps God is

strong enough to exult in monotony. It is possible that God says every morning, "Do it again" to the sun; and every evening, "Do it again" to the moon.[14]

I suspect that curiosity and wonder differ in their questions. The curious one questions in order to possess, or to show off. Ultimately, the curious ask questions for themselves. The wonderer asks questions they don't already know the answers to.[15] They delight in someone else knowing. Like the widow to the unjust judge, or the hungry child to their father, the wonderer asks out of genuine desire. They ask because they long for truth. You might say that they pray.

STUDY AS PRAYER

If all our knowing is only participating in what God already knows, how could our study *not* involve prayer? What would our questions be, and how would our questions change if we asked them to God?

Theologian Fred Sanders points out that God asks a lot of questions in the Bible. In the Gospels alone, Jesus asks dozens of questions to His followers. And Christians over the years have asked plenty of questions in return. Have you considered Augustine's *Confessions*, asks Sanders? The first few pages contain thirty-seven questions!

> Since Augustine is praying to God in response to God's own words, spoken in Scripture, spoken preveniently before Augustine responds, and spoken so plentifully that they are inexhaustibly deep, why would we expect him to ever run out of questions for God? . . . Why would that come to an end, if God is the God of the living?[16]

When our questions are responding to God's own questions, when our study is done in pursuit of the good, the true, and the beautiful, it becomes prayer.

If you're like me, and you succeeded at school by keeping one eye on grades and the professor's approval, it's quite a change to begin to pray your questions. You can't think your way out of a rut. You need practices, tangible things to help.

Bruce Hindmarsh once encouraged me to keep a candle on my desk, and light it whenever I begin to read or write. The lit candle works as a sign, a visible reminder, that I do my work in the presence of the Lord. My work should be done for Him, not for anything I can get out of it. My study becomes prayer, and I bring my questions, doubts, and anxieties to the One who already knows everything.

If every Christian is called to the studious life, and this life is characterized by attention, wonder, and prayer, then we'll learn to live it by emulating those who've gone before: Paula, Cassiodorus, Timothy I.

What better way to imitate these studious saints than by learning their prayers? As we begin our studies, we might echo this prayer of Anselm:

> O Lord my God. Teach my heart this day where and how to find you.
>
> You have made me and re-made me, and you have bestowed on me all the good things I possess,
>
> and still I do not know you. I have not yet done that for which I was made.
>
> Teach me to seek you, for I cannot seek you unless you teach me,
>
> or find you unless you show yourself to me.

Let me seek you in my desire; let me desire you in my seeking.

Let me find you by loving you; let me love you when I find you.[17]

Almighty God, you have knit together your elect in one communion and fellowship in the mystical Body of your Son: Give us grace so to follow your blessed saints in all virtuous and godly living, that we may come to those ineffable joys that you have prepared for those who truly love you; through Jesus Christ our Lord, who with you and the Holy Spirit lives and reigns, one God, in glory everlasting. Amen.

Collect for All Saints' Day,
the *Book of Common Prayer*

8

Our Inheritance
Receiving the Gift of Tradition

Imagine a man who has lived his whole life in the wilderness, in complete isolation. Let's call him Tom. Tom has grown up entirely alone, untouched by civilization and community. He's a forager—he's only ever eaten the roots and mushrooms and berries he finds in the wild.

But one day, out of nowhere, Tom stumbles across Julia Child's recipe for beef bourguignon. It's a fantastic recipe, adapting high French cuisine so the ordinary American home cook might pull it off—something I've done approximately half the times I've tried.

But when Tom reads the recipe he is, of course, completely befuddled. To someone who has lived on forage, the recipe may as well be written in French. Step one instructs, "Simmer bacon rind." What does that mean? To answer this question, you have to know something about pigs, and about how to kill them and cut them up, and about which parts are tasty and which are not. You also have to know about fire, and cast iron, and skillets, and how to combine parts of pigs with skillets and fire in the right proportion and for the right length of time so you end up with simmered bacon. He's only on step one of ten and Tom is already hopelessly stuck.

LEARNING TO COOK: TRADITION AS FREEDOM

No one could ever learn to cook entirely on their own. Cooking is a basic human activity, something all humans do. But cooking is necessarily cultural and social, and as such, it requires belonging to a tradition. In fact, that's understating it: Cooking requires belonging to *many* traditions.

Left to himself, how is Tom to dine on whatever he wants? The question is an absurdity. Without the wisdom, practices, and artifacts that make up a culinary tradition, Tom is more than limited. He is utterly unable to cook; he couldn't make a grilled cheese sandwich, let alone a magnificent beef stew.

So let's give Tom some more tradition. He already has the recipe, itself the fruit of a vibrant, long-running culinary culture. Let's introduce him to a pig farmer. He belongs to a long tradition of animal husbandry, those heroes who first caught, then bred, then carefully cultivated wild hogs into something glorious. Thanks to them we enjoy bacon. Let's introduce Tom to a blacksmith, who belongs to another tradition that stretches back thousands of years to some intrepid soul who figured out how to melt crude iron and steel and pour them into a sand mold. Without any tradition, Tom would never be able to "simmer the bacon rind." But give him bacon and a cast iron pot, and step one is easy.

We could go through the rest of the recipe, step by step—but you get the point. Just for Tom to enjoy his morning bacon, he must draw on centuries of tradition—entire fields of expertise, an array of crafts and technologies, a wealth of finely tuned cultural practices. Without tradition, the best he can do is roots and berries. And that's probably too optimistic: Which mushrooms or berries will kill you?

Without tradition, Tom would be better off as an undomesticated wild hog, who at least has instincts and a sharp sense of smell.

Tradition is bound up, not only in cooking, but in everything that makes our lives human.

TRADITION AIN'T WHAT IT USED TO BE

"Think for yourself." I bet you've heard this advice before. "Make up your own mind!" Don't be influenced by others, push out all tradition and custom, go with whatever you find inside your own head.

This notion is thoroughly debunked by Alan Jacobs in *How to Think*. First of all, Jacobs points out, "thinking for yourself" is not possible, as we're social beings and thus social thinkers. And if it were possible it would be terrible. It would produce very bad thinking—just as trying to make beef bourguignon by "thinking for yourself" would produce very bad stew.

The problem with "think for yourself" is that it fails to recognize that not only our *thought* but nearly all that makes life good and beautiful involves tradition.

When it comes to theology, however, tradition gets trickier. For Protestants, it can be a word that sets off alarm bells. Tradition? Isn't that what some churches rely on instead of sticking to the Bible? Isn't that the man-made, human stuff—unreliable, flawed, easily corrupted?

If Protestants tend to be suspicious of tradition, all the more the inheritors of the eighteenth-century Enlightenment. "Dare to know!" exclaimed Immanual Kant. "Have the courage to use your own understanding."[1] (Think for yourself!) By the lights of modernity, tradition is stifling, dogmatic, lifeless. It's unresponsive to the dynamic complexity of reality. As every Disney cartoon preaches, only those who courageously reject tradition will become their authentic selves.

Another critique of tradition sees it as backward looking. Isn't tradition just another word for nostalgia? For the idea that things used to be perfect, or that conventions should never change? Our cultural moment is increasingly critical of the past, certain that anyone who looks to history for wisdom must be sexist, racist, or at best, naïve. As the late great humorist Peter De Vries put it, "Nostalgia ain't what it used to be."[2]

Even as I raise these critiques levied against tradition by various Protestants, modern philosophers, and contemporary activists, you already have reason to question them. You know that tradition is more—otherwise you wouldn't buy and read books, and here you are. So how do we rescue the idea of tradition?

LEARNING TO PAINT: THE CREATIVITY OF TRADITION

Part of our problem is confusing *tradition* with *traditionalism*. We sometimes think tradition means nostalgia for a supposedly lost "golden age." But Jaroslav Pelikan, eminent church historian, argues why this is wrong: "Tradition is the living faith of the dead; traditionalism is the dead faith of the living." Tradition is a disciplined mode of thought, Pelikan explains; it is thinking *with* rather than *against* history.[3]

> "Tradition is the living faith of the dead; traditionalism is the dead faith of the living."

What does this mean? How might we think *with* history?

This is a question that Roman Catholic theologians have also wrestled with. For some Catholics, tradition means an uncritical, blind acceptance of what has been. But for Catholic theologian Yves Congar, the church's tradition is much more alive and dynamic.

Consider learning how to paint. The beginning artist must, of course, first learn and mimic the form of master painters. But, Congar explains, his end goal is not to become exceptional at imitating what came before. The artist learns the masters, Congar concluded, "to continue their creative work in its original spirit, which thus, in a new generation, is born again with the freedom, the youthfulness and the promise that it originally possessed."[4]

We often oppose creativity and tradition. We imagine creativity as the lack of constraint and limitation, as crossing boundaries and breaking conventions. This misconception is founded on a prior mistake—thinking of freedom as primarily a negation. Freedom, we typically think, is "freedom from." But this is not true for the artist, who seeks "freedom *for*" something. The artist finds freedom when she has been formed in her craft such that she can image forth truth, goodness, and beauty.

In other words, belonging to a tradition opens up the artist to genuine creativity, insight, and freedom. Our foraging friend Tom isn't free to cook when left to his own devices; he *becomes* more free, he becomes *able* to be creative, when he is given a culinary tradition.

If this is true for the artist, and the chef, what about the theologian?

PASSING ON THE FAITH

One of the most poignant parts of the New Testament is Paul's second letter to Timothy. Imprisoned in Rome, awaiting his trial and execution, Paul has time to reflect. He remembers those who have gone before: his faithful ancestors, and Lois and Eunice, who passed on their faith to Timothy. He then exhorts Timothy, "Follow the pattern of the sound words that you have heard from me." "Guard the good deposit entrusted to you." He is concerned with what has been delivered to Timothy by himself, Lois, and Eunice.

Then Paul looks forward. He tells Timothy, "What you have heard from me in the presence of many witnesses entrust to faithful men who will be able to teach others also." The sequence extends: ancestors, grandmother, mother, Paul, Timothy, the next generation, the one after. (See 2 Tim.1:13, 14; 2:2 ESV.)

In a very real way, you and I heard the gospel preached because Timothy, and those after him, and those after them, did exactly what Paul urged. They passed on the faith—which is to say, they *traditioned*.

> Some difficulty comes from assuming that Scripture and tradition are entirely separate categories.

That's what the word means. It comes from the Latin *tradere*, which means something like "passing on." The Greek equivalent is *paradidonai*: "handing over," "to deliver," or "the giving." Tradition is a gift, and the gift in question is the apostolic witness to Christ.

This touches on another common misconception. Because of long-standing arguments between Catholics and Protestants, we tend to think of Scripture and tradition as competing authorities. *Sola scriptura* or *Scripture and tradition*? I can't solve those debates in these pages, but it's worth pointing out that some of the difficulty comes from assuming that Scripture and tradition are entirely separate categories.

Think back to Paul's letter to Timothy. We read this letter today because it has been passed down—it has been *traditioned*. None of us stumbled onto the Christian Scriptures out of the blue; the Bible didn't drop out of the sky—we didn't find it in the woods like Tom's recipe. Instead, these inspired texts have been "delivered," passed down over the centuries by faithful pastors, booksellers, translators, missionaries, scribes, mothers and fathers—all of whom played a part in handing on the apostolic witness.

This means that Scripture is at the heart of Christian tradition. The Bible, godly preaching, catechisms, sacred art and poetry, the stories of the saints, the wisdom of theologians, the judicious judgments of church councils—all of this has been passed down. Tradition, in other words, names the normative way in which Christ has built His church. *Tradere*, "passing on," is how the vast majority of Christians throughout time and around the world have come to faith in Christ.

One of our Brazos Fellows alumni, Mitchell, told me about a question he got from a friend: "Why would I read a theologian when I could just read God's Word?" Why not just stick to the Bible? Fair question.

Mitchell replied, "In that case, why even tell me about what you're reading in the Bible?" We're meant to hear God's Word alongside one another. The Bible comes to *us*, not just to *me*. As Mitchell put it, "Reading a theologian is to be in conversation with fellow Christians—who are also learning to love God in their time and place." This is tradition: the church, throughout time and around the world, in an extended conversation about what God has spoken to us.

DIVINE GENEROSITY: THE MESS AND MYSTERY OF TRADITION

This account of tradition might seem overly optimistic. So let's be clear: There's a good deal of mess involved. It's not only good things we've inherited, but also plenty that is flawed, ugly, and untrue. In my research as a historian of American religion, I study ways in which tradition has been misused, including by the nineteenth-century defenders of chattel slavery.

Anyone who has studied church history knows that it's frequently a real mess. And that's because people just like you and me are involved.

The mess isn't new—it's not unique to the contemporary church in America, or late medieval Catholicism, or Constantine's day. It's throughout the story of God's people. It's messy in the Old Testament and the New. It's messy when the apostles are literally rubbing shoulders with Jesus. It's certainly messy in the church we read of in the Acts of the Apostles. But for all the flaws and foibles and genuine tragedies of this story, the passing on, the handing over, is the primary means by which Christ has built His church.

> **Apparently, God delights in making partners out of flawed people like us.**

Apparently, God *likes* to do things this way. He doesn't need to, but God delights in bringing us into the story—He takes pleasure in making partners out of flawed, shortsighted, selfish people like you and me.

Think about it: After hanging out with the Twelve for years, Christ still leaves things in their hands. Couldn't He have just stuck around and proclaimed His resurrection Himself? Wouldn't that have been much more efficient? Much less messy?

But a beautiful thing about our God is that His triune life is always and eternally overflowing with generosity. *God loves sharing.* In creation, God shares in His very being; in redemption, God adopts us so that we share in His Sonship and can call Him Father. And then God invites and empowers us, through His Spirit, to participate in His divine mission. Tradition, in other words, is just a way of naming how God loves to work not *around* but *through* us.

I'm a big fan of the Buffalo Bills, so I'll ask you to tolerate a football analogy. Picture quarterback Josh Allen, a hero among men, leading the Bills on a game-winning drive. All the way down the field, he is doing amazing Josh Allen things: stiff-arming linemen, leaping over defenders, throwing perfect completions while on the run. Finally, on fourth-and-goal from the one yard line, instead of diving into the end zone he tosses the ball to a wide-open offensive tackle who lined up as an eligible receiver. Josh could score himself, and he did all the real work getting the team down the field. But he loves letting the backup tackle score the touchdown.

Let me be clear: Although I really like Josh Allen, this is nonetheless a very inadequate analogy. God's power and goodness and generosity are incomparably greater, and our participation is entirely dependent on God's grace. But although small and dependent, our part is *nonetheless* a *genuine participation*. We get to be part of the play even though God has no need of us. He delights in bringing us in, if you will, to catch that pass.

The mystery of tradition is that it reveals the generosity and faithfulness of God even when we flounder and fail. Christ promised to build His church, and He has not failed to keep His word. From those first few hundreds who heard and saw Jesus to several billions of believers around the world today, God has worked through His followers to draw a people to Himself. The story of the church is a story of God's faithfulness expressed *through tradition*. We'll know better who we are, and what we ought to do, if we remember that this is our story.

REMEMBER THESE WORDS: INHABITING THE TRADITION

So how might we do this? How might we more fully inhabit this story? What might we learn by remembering how the faith has been passed on? Let me suggest three ways you can do this as part of your common rule:

First, grow in gratitude by tracing your story through the tradition. In my desk drawer is a hand-drawn genealogy from my grandfather, a map of my dad's family back to the Old World. During the chaos of the mid-nineteenth-century revolutions in Europe, Frederick N. Gutacker emigrated from Hesse, Germany, to western New York, where he met a cute Catholic girl and converted so they could marry. His two Lutheran brothers never spoke to him again. We pass on this family history because it tells us who we are.

The desire to know our stories is stronger than ever. We're obsessed with ancestry; we use new research tools, subscribe to digital records, and test our DNA to figure out what percentage of us is Scottish or Icelandic or Portuguese. All of this reflects a deep desire to know our roots. Where did I come from? Who are my people?

What about our spiritual genealogy? At the start of the Brazos Fellows year I ask each fellow:

How did you come to know the Lord?

Who told you? Who told them?

What churches did you grow up in? What churches were home to those who told you?

Who planted those churches?

It's interesting how far back some of the fellows can trace their spiritual family tree—how, when, and where their parents, grandparents, even great-grandparents came to faith.

I wonder what you might find if you spent even an hour on Google exploring your Christian genealogy. You might trace people and churches back through the last century, further back to the denominations that grew during the Second Great Awakening; with some luck you could trace those communities back to Europe, perhaps to the era of Reformations; if you get that far, you could theoretically follow threads back through Christendom, the expansion of the gospel during the Middle Ages, back into the patristic era and, finally, to the apostles.

Whoever introduced you to Christ, however the faith was passed on to you, the genealogy could *at least in theory* be traced person-to-person, church-to-church, all the way back to those who walked and ate and lived with Jesus. If you did this, what you'd be mapping is tradition—the passing on of the faith that Paul describes. It's how you got here—you belong to a line that stretches all the way back to the imprisoned apostle.

What might be the spiritual benefit of this exercise? Of finding your story in the tradition?

How might it renew your gratitude to God for His faithfulness over the centuries?

Second, grow in humility by reading old books. In the 1940s, C. S. Lewis worried about the modern propensity toward "chronological snobbery," or what he called "the uncritical acceptance of the intellectual climate common to our own age."[5] What corrects this? Lewis argued that the cure was "to keep the clean sea breeze of the centuries blowing through our minds, and this can be done only by reading old books."[6]

These lines are quoted all over the place, and rightly so. But it's not where Lewis starts:

> There is a strange idea abroad that in every subject the ancient books should be read only by the professionals, and that the amateur should content himself with the modern books. Thus I have found as a tutor in English Literature that if the average student wants to find out something about Platonism, the very last thing he thinks of doing is to take a translation of Plato off the library shelf and read the Symposium. He would rather read some dreary modern book ten times as long, all about "isms" and influences and only once in twelve pages telling him what Plato actually said.[7]

Lewis's point is that old books are for *amateurs*, not just professionals. And, in particular, old books of Christian *theology*—like the new translation of St. Athanasius' *On the Incarnation* he's introducing. He celebrates how the translator made Athanasius more accessible to "the world at large, not only . . . theological students." He hopes that it will inspire other translations, since laypeople need to read not only summaries of theology, or devotional works, but also classic works of doctrine. Lewis argues that reading the theological tradition is for ordinary Christians, not just academics or clergy.

And one benefit of doing this is growing in humility. Reading *On the Incarnation*, as Lewis says, chastens our chronological snobbery. Athanasius is not interested in the same questions that you and I are; he doesn't care about the latest argument on social media. Reading him pulls us out of the myopia of the present moment.

Reading the tradition also encourages humility simply by being hard. A book like *On the Incarnation* is not quickly grasped and digested. It is difficult; we don't read it once and feel we've mastered the text. And, when we remember the extraordinary sanctity of the author—Athanasius was exiled five times for defending orthodoxy—we are compelled not to approach the work as a critic but to let it judge us.

> **What might we learn from the difficult work of reading classic works of theology?**

What might we learn from the difficult work of reading classic works of theology? How might we be stretched, challenged? How might we grow in humility as we learn from those who have gone before us?

Third, grow in courage by learning the lives of the saints. Growing up, there was a vast, blank space in my sense of the past—a great gap between the New Testament and my church (with the exception of Martin Luther). But as I started to study church history, that empty space became populated by names and stories.

I learned about the heroic second-century mothers Perpetua and Felicity, who bravely faced their martyrdom in the arena; the incorrigible Athanasius and his defense of Christ's divinity; the generous Basil the Great, who founded the world's first hospital to care for the poor; the wise Gregory the Great, whose leadership saved the people of Rome and helped spread the gospel to the pagans; the pioneering Cyril and Methodius, who brought the faith to the Slavic east. These and others began to populate the "great cloud of witnesses" in my imagination.

We can't live without heroes, whether fictional superheroes, the American Founding Fathers, athletes, actors, celebrity pastors, or self-help gurus. The question is not whether or not we'll be formed by examples. The question is whether or not, when we find ourselves following our heroes, we are also following Christ.

Learning the lives of the saints puts before us heroes we should want to be like. As the apostle Paul put it to the church in 1 Corinthians 11, "Be imitators of me, as I am of Christ." How do we learn to follow Christ? By following those who followed Him.

It's easy to take tradition for granted. Few of us feel deeply grateful every time we pull bacon out of our fridge, turn on our stove, and toss some strips into a cast-iron pan. Just cooking breakfast requires a remarkably rich, diverse set of culinary traditions and technologies. If we lived without them for any length of time, we'd quickly notice; if we somehow grew up without them entirely, like Tom, they would astound us.

And this is only to speak of one kind of tradition. What about language itself? Think of the stories, the songs, the poetry and literature, the jokes, the expressions of love, the prayers that we inherit.

Our very identity—everything involved in how we make meaning, understand the world and ourselves, relate to others—depends on what's been passed down.

Our lives are enriched by tradition in ways we can never grasp.

This is also true of our Christian lives. We have inherited so much: the riches of Scripture, Christian theological, literary, devotional, and poetic work, hymnody and sacred music, art and architecture, the lives of the saints. We find ourselves at a table laden with a feast that we did not prepare. The table bows under the weight of it.

How will you receive the gift that is this feast?

Blessed Lord, who caused all Holy Scriptures to be written for our learning: Grant us so to hear them, read, mark, learn, and inwardly digest them, that by patience and the comfort of your Holy Word we may embrace and ever hold fast the blessed hope of everlasting life, which you have given us in our Savior Jesus Christ; who lives and reigns with you and the Holy Spirit, one God, for ever and ever. Amen.

Collect for the Second Sunday of Advent, the *Book of Common Prayer*

9

Practicing Reading Together

I'll never forget the first time I read the poetry of George Herbert—or, rather, the first time I heard it. At evening prayer one Wednesday, an elderly professor named Ralph Wood gave a short talk on "Love III," one of the more famous poems by the seventeenth-century priest. The poem begins:

> Love bade me welcome. Yet my soul drew back
> > Guilty of dust and sin.
> But quick-eyed Love, observing me grow slack
> > From my first entrance in,
> Drew nearer to me, sweetly questioning,
> > If I lacked any thing.

What I lacked was an appreciation for poetry. As an undergrad, after watching the *Dead Poets Society*, I realized that being into poetry was very cool. But I had little experience and, frankly, not much patience for it. Sitting there listening to Herbert, I wanted to hear more.

Dr. Wood went on to winsomely explicate the poem, which features Herbert at his witty best. The speaker, a shamefaced guest, refuses the invitation of Love. He's all too serious about his unworthiness, but his host makes a pun: "Love took my hand, and smiling did reply, / Who made the eyes but I?" Love, as Dr. Wood put it, likes a joke. (Did you hear the pun?)

By the time Dr. Wood finished, I was transformed, transfixed by this vision of Christ's self-giving hospitality to me, the undeserving guest. I was also newly in love with Herbert.

Several times in the years that followed, I had the chance to sit around the table with Dr. Wood and the Brazos Fellows to read George Herbert together. Herbert is not an extravagant poet—he doesn't play with sound like Gerard Manley Hopkins or soar to dramatic heights like John Donne. But his deceptively simple poems hold a trove of riches.

I tell this story not to endorse reading Herbert (though please do) but to make a confession: On my own, I saw only a fraction of what was in his poems. Few things have been as good for my humility as reading poetry with other people. It's an exercise in realizing just how much I miss.

Put more positively, poetry is meant to be read with others. This isn't unique to poetry; it only appears more obvious than with other kinds of reading. We see more when we don't see on our own.

If we're all called to the studious life, reading together is the best way to begin. Reading together helps us grow in prayer as we give voice to our longings, doubts, and fears. Reading together helps us grow in wonder as we ask new questions. Reading together helps us grow in gratitude as we reencounter truths that have become too familiar.

Reading together, in sum, cultivates studiousness. And since it's part of the common rule you're considering, we need to get practical. *Who* should we read with? *What* might we read together? And *how* should we read—what practices and habits make our reading together fruitful?

DON'T THINK FOR YOURSELF . . .

If Alan Jacobs is right, then our question changes from "How can I think entirely on my own, apart from anyone else's influence?" to "Whom should I think *with*?"[1]

What makes a good thinking partner? By what criteria would you decide? What makes someone *trustworthy* to think with?

Jacobs suggests that more important than *like-mindedness* is *like-heartedness*, those who "are temperamentally disposed to openness and have habits of listening."[2] Good thinking partners care more about the truth than proving a point or showing themselves to be smart. They readily admit when they've missed something. They're willing to wonder.

But the friend of truth also avoids the opposite mistake: prioritizing peace above all else. Sometimes, we overreact to belligerent "truth-tellers." We start to think that kindness means nodding along or keeping quiet. At its worst, this takes the form of mutual flattery, which works like a corrosive on genuine friendship.

Both extremes—let's call them showy argumentativeness and people-pleasing passivity—result in a disordered relationship toward the truth. Both fail to care properly about truth and, to the same extent, to care about the other person.

There's no blueprint for exactly how, on every topic, in every circumstance and relationship, we ought to "speak the truth in love." Understanding how and when to do this takes prudence, which takes maturity.

In the meanwhile, we can aspire to be friends both with each other and with truth. We can seek out those who aren't prone to argumentativeness, passivity, or flattery. And, as part of your common rule, you and your friends can work at this. You can commit to speak, think, and read together in ways that are friendly toward the truth.

. . . THINK WITH THE CHURCH

The last two chapters have invited you to embrace your calling as a lifelong student and to receive the gift of tradition. These come together in another invitation: to think with the church. If your aim is to grow in holy wisdom, to more deeply encounter truth, ask your questions *with* and *to* the people of God.

What might this look like when it comes to reading?

How might you and your community practice *thinking with* the church?

First, read Scripture with the church. While every Christian can and should study the Bible, these Scriptures did not come directly from God to you. Rather, Scripture has been received, acknowledged, preserved, taught, and passed on by a community.

Christians of various denominations differ on what this means for our interpretation. But most agree that we shouldn't ignore how the church has received and read the Bible. As biblical scholar Craig Allert puts it, "The church certainly has something to say about what the Bible says because the Bible is the church's book."[3]

Listening along as the church reads Scripture helps our own reading: It illuminates our personal or cultural blind spots. It corrects our imbalances, challenges our assumptions. It enlivens our reading, as we notice afresh things that have become familiar. Putting the Bible under the light of the church is like slowly turning a gemstone to reflect facet after facet, illuminating its inexhaustible beauty.

How might you read Scripture with the church? Consider one of these approaches:

- Read a psalm alongside sermons or commentaries. Augustine's *Expositions on the Psalms*[4] and Hilary's *Homilies on the Psalms*[5] are free online, while many others can be purchased, such as sermons by the twelfth-century monk Bernard of Clairvaux.[6] Practice a slow, layered rereading: the psalm first, then Augustine, then the psalm, then Bernard, then the psalm again.

- Pick a book of the Bible to study, with each member reading a commentary from different eras and traditions. For example, read the Acts of the Apostles alongside commentaries by the fourth-century archbishop John Chrysostom, the Slavic-American church historian Jaroslav Pelikan, evangelical biblical scholar Holly Beers, and African American theologian Willie James Jennings.

- Consider splurging on a volume of the *Ancient Christian Commentary on Scripture* (a paperback costs about $50). Each volume collects brief selections from early Christian theologians on a biblical book, offering a remarkable panoply of interpretation. (If your pastor or priest owns the series, perhaps they'd loan you a volume.)

- For another angle, check out the Visual Commentary on Scripture, an online resource that brings ancient, medieval, modern, and contemporary art into dialogue around particular stories of Scripture.[7]

As you read the Bible along with these commentators, artists, and saints, ask, What do they notice? What do they hear? How might the same Spirit who inspired the holy text be working through these saints to illuminate your reading?

Second, read the theological tradition of the church. We live with an incredible opportunity: Never has the church enjoyed greater access to the wisdom of those who went before us. From free commentaries online, to well-curated book series, to cheap used books (the

Complete Poems of George Herbert is the cost of a pumpkin spice latte), it's never been easier to immerse in the Great Tradition.

But we rarely take advantage of this accessibility. Perhaps we don't know where to start or we feel intimidated. Wouldn't Julian of Norwich's *Revelations of Divine Love* be too confusing? Wouldn't it be arduous to work through Augustine's *Confessions*? Wouldn't it be more efficient to just read a summary, scan the SparkNotes?

Or maybe, if we're honest, we don't have much of an appetite for this kind of reading. And, to be sure, reading old books *can* be difficult. It takes time and effort to engage the philosophical reasoning of an Augustinian treatise, the allusions of a Dante canto, or the spiritual vision of a Christina Rossetti poem. Most evenings we'd rather watch or listen or skim the latest show, podcast, or social media feed.

> **Reading old books can be difficult. That's part of the point. The time we have to give them allows these books to work on us.**

There's nothing wrong with a bit of light reading or entertainment. But what makes a fine snack makes a terrible diet. The more we fill up on "junk food," the more we lose our appetite for anything that asks more of us.

And the difficulty of classic texts is not a problem to be solved but part of the point. The time they require allows these books to work on us. They stretch our capacity—and we need stretching. They offer gentle resistance, asking that we give ourselves to them before we understand.

This can be difficult and humbling. But there's plenty of help available—you don't have to plod through it on your own. Here are a few ways to dive into the Great Tradition:

Read primary sources—especially in clear translations, and especially those with helpful introductions. Exemplary on both counts is the Popular Patristics Series published by St. Vladimir's Seminary Press.[8] Jump in with Athanasius' *On the Incarnation* or *Tertullian, Cyprian, and Origen On the Lord's Prayer.*

After, during, or before reading the primary sources, read the best works about them. Buy Robert Louis Wilken's *The Spirit of Early Christian Thought*. It's masterful, accessible, and devotional—a great introduction to the Christian theological tradition.

The *Holy Joys* project has put together a free guide, a yearlong survey of patristic theology.[9]

Take advantage of other free guides to the classics. Jessica Hooten Wilson's YouTube channel offers help reading Dostoevsky, O'Connor, Eliot, Chesterton, and more. Likewise, *Close Reads*, a "book club podcast," features great discussions of classics old and new. The *100 Days of Dante* project is an incredible series of videos that walk you through the *Divine Comedy*.

Most importantly: Don't go it alone.

Third, read the tradition with other Christians. Every year, I have the privilege of sitting around a table with ordinary Christians, from varied backgrounds and with different training, who for the first time are reading Athanasius, Julian, and Dante. Time and again, I've watched the Brazos Fellows help each other read fruitfully. This has left me increasingly convinced that the Great Tradition is for everybody—we're all invited to pull up a chair to this table.

Talking with others about anything you're reading is fruitful. But it's especially so with difficult books, and even more with classics from the Christian tradition. Each of us notices different things, understands or is confused by different things, is disturbed or intrigued by different things. Together, we see more.

And something particularly special happens when we read the Christian Scriptures and tradition together. When we read the work of saints, we welcome our brother or sister in Christ to continue speaking. As Alan Jacobs puts it, "the dead, being dead, speak only at our invitation: they will not come uninvited to our table."[10] By reading, discussing, and questioning their work, we give voice to those who have gone before. We act out a theological truth: We share with them in the communion of the saints.[11]

> By reading, discussing, and questioning old works, we give voice to those who would otherwise be silenced by the grave.

This is a truth that fortifies us when reading gets difficult. When you struggle to understand, imagine how wonderful (and strange!) it would be to sit around the table with Basil the Great, Dorothy Sayers, and Catherine of Siena. What an honor to listen to and learn from these saints. If Christ tarries, in a thousand years Christians will still be at it, sitting around a table somewhere, trying their best to understand Dante or Julian. It's been going on for centuries and will continue until the end of time. For now, it's our turn: We get to be here, taking part in this ongoing conversation between the living and the dead.

LEARNING TO WONDER: SHARING THE INTELLECTUAL LIFE

So we ought to think *with* the church—to read Scripture and the tradition, and to do so together. But if that answers the "who" and "what," now it's time to talk about the "how." How do we do this well? What are practices and habits of reading—and discussing—that cultivate wonder? And how might you make such study a part of your common rule?

Study: Practicing Reading Together

Over a decade of teaching undergrad and graduate students, leading tutorials, and being a grad student myself, I've gathered some practical advice on reading that applies broadly. Here are a few rules I've found personally helpful:

First, read with intention. I often find myself staring at a paragraph for a while, picking up a few phrases, turning the page ... after an hour of this my eyes may have passed over the text, but I haven't really read it. Instead, be clear to yourself what you're up to. If you can say *why* you're reading, and *what* you're looking for, it's easier to avoid mindlessly staring at the book. Take a moment before you begin to express what you're wondering. Why am I reading this? What am I looking for? What do I want to understand, and why might this author help me?

Second, keep the book's big picture in mind. This starts with what the author says is most important. Pay close attention to the title of the work, as well as chapter titles, headings, and subheadings. Each of these is a signpost for what the author (and/or translator or editor) thinks matters most. Likewise, the beginnings and endings of each chapter often clearly state or summarize the main point. These provide a guide for what to look for.

Third, underline and annotate with extravagance. The more you engage as you read, the better. Wonder with your pencil: Underline phrases or ideas that strike you, put "?" or "!" in the margin next to bits that surprise or confuse, jot down key quotes or questions that the text raises. At the end, try to summarize the big ideas in your own words. This takes discipline, but even taking two minutes to write down a few sentences about what you've just read is worthwhile.

Fourth, talk out loud about it. Grab your roommate or the barista, your work colleague or a church friend and try, in sixty seconds, to summarize what you just read. Take a stab at articulating why it might be important, why it raises significant questions. Voice your questions or what confused you. We better remember things when we say them out loud.

Once you've done this work, and gathered together around the table or living room, what then? What practices contribute to truly thinking together? What makes for a good discussion?

Here are my few suggestions:

Don't start with criticism. We're all tempted to appear intelligent by criticizing, by tearing apart an argument. But while a healthy discussion often involves questioning and disagreeing with an author, it's usually not the best place to begin. Above all, avoid opening with "What did you like or not like?" Instead, begin by each sharing something that surprised or delighted you, or a genuine question the text raised. Or, even better:

Open with a big question. A small question about a text is "What did you like?" or "Is author X right about issue Y?" A big question is "What kind of transformation does Dante undergo in *Purgatorio*?" or "Why does Julian of Norwich tell that parable?" or "How can you tell if a revival is really a work of the Spirit?" A big question is one you could talk about for hours—it's a question motivated by wonder.[12]

Listen to each other—like, actually. We've all been in "discussions" that were just a group of people taking turns talking past each other. This is because actually listening is quite difficult—remember chapter 2? Commit to wait several moments after each comment before someone responds. While someone else is speaking you won't be flipping through the text, thinking of your next remark—you'll be hearing what they say.

Give space for reflection. Once or twice during a discussion, allow extended time for gathering thoughts and questions. A discussion doesn't have to be unbroken speech—it can involve deliberate silence and stillness. Take three minutes for everyone to look through their text and notes, and then bring new thoughts back to the discussion.

Stay grounded in the text. Any great work evokes thoughts and questions that extend beyond what the author wrote. Exploring these tangents can be deeply rewarding. But the author and their work deserve to be taken on their own terms. At *least* for the first half of a discussion, stick to what the author meant. You can tell whether you're doing this if, after a comment, you can answer the question, "Where do you see that in the text?"

Don't ever "finish." The sorts of texts we're talking about are never mastered—you could spend a lifetime in their company and not exhaust them. Take time at the end of a discussion to name the questions you're left with. What's a new thought you want to keep considering? What are you still wrestling with? What do you wonder after this conversation? These are ways of extending rather than ending the discussion.

SAYING NO: DISTRACTIONS AND DEVICES

In order to say yes to studiousness we have to say no to something else. What negation is required? What might you need to say no to if you want to read well?

The single hardest thing about study is distraction. Even as I write this paragraph, I'm aware of a device on my desk crafted to capture my attention. And it just worked: The darn thing buzzed, and since I've been so well trained, I paused typing to see what just came in.

By now, I think we all know that our digital technologies do this. Our devices easily rob us of the riches we only find with sustained attention. So what do we do?

When it comes to screens, how do you need to say no? You could get really radical by abandoning your smartphone. Or take my friend Matt Anderson's advice: Quit Netflix.[13] Seriously, consider taking drastic measures. If you really want to go deeper—both in your friendships and in your study—one of the best things you can do is convince your friends to join you in taking a year off from streaming services and social media. You won't regret it. At a minimum, pull back from screen time, taking back space from social media, TV, podcasts, and so on. The more you say no to these things, the more you'll be able to say yes to attentive reading.

Here are a few other simple nos that might help:[14]

Don't try to multitask. The research is quite clear. If you think you can multitask, study after study shows that you're wrong. You absorb less, reread the same lines, and remember almost nothing. So instead of two hours "reading" while keeping one eye on the sports game, listening to music, or periodically checking Facebook, spend half of that time *just reading.*

Banish screens. By far, the number one way to improve your reading is do it without a screen at hand. Ideally, read with your phone, tablet, laptop, TV in another room entirely. (The benefits of screen-free reading extend to reading physical books, by the way.[15]) And having done this, you'll need to ...

Embrace the technologies of pen and paper. This means accepting both the limitations of handwriting *and* its unique opportunities. Different parts of your brain light up when you write by hand than when you type; you literally think different thoughts. And you'll want to have paper notes for your discussion, because you will ...

Install a phone basket. We talked about this in chapter 3. When you gather to discuss (and to eat; and especially to pray), put a basket by the door with a friendly invitation: "Leave your phone here and be with us!"

GETTING STARTED WITH READING TOGETHER

So you've decided to study together. As part of your common rule, you'll read and discuss and seek to better know the truth. How do you begin? Where to start?

First, pick a book you've heard good things about—perhaps one of the texts mentioned above. This can be a group decision every time, or you can take turns picking the next read. See the reading lists under further resources later in the book for reading plan ideas.

Next, find a format that works best for reading and meeting. Do you want "bite-sized" discussions in which you read a chapter or two and meet once a week? Or to read more and meet biweekly? Might you meet monthly to discuss a whole book? If possible, pick a time other than your weekly communal meal. Otherwise, either your community time or your discussion (most likely the latter) will get short shrift.

What's most important is committing as a group to a plan you'll stick with. Recognize that this study involves a real commitment. When somebody doesn't do the reading, or doesn't show up, they're not the only one who misses out—the whole group misses their perspective.

After a set amount of time, reevaluate. What's going well? What might work better? What small changes could you make to the time, duration, location of the meeting, or the type of reading that might help?

As with all great poems, you're allowed to read "Love III" more than one way. You might read it eucharistically: Christ serves us at the table and invites us to "taste my meat." You might also read "Love

III" as an invitation to studiousness. Love welcomes us to a table where, through good reading and charitable discussion, we feast intellectually and spiritually. We're invited to savor the words of sacred Scripture, to imbibe the wisdom of the body of Christ, the Great Tradition.

For those of us who feel ourselves holding back, who feel unworthy (surely *I'm* not clever or well-educated enough), smiling Love reminds us, "Who made the mind but I?" All that we lack will be made up by our gracious host. All that's left for us to do is sit and eat.

Discern: Learning to Attend

PART FOUR

Preparing to Die: Living Our Vocation

Hearing His Voice: The Lifelong Project of Discernment

Practicing Sabbath

Almighty God, whose most dear Son went not up to joy but first he suffered pain, and entered not into glory before he was crucified: Mercifully grant that we, walking in the way of the Cross, may find it none other than the way of life and peace; through Jesus Christ your Son our Lord. Amen.

Collect for Endurance,
the *Book of Common Prayer*

10

Preparing to Die
Living Our Vocation

Are you looking for a job? Unsure what career path to take? Allow me to pitch a highly selective career you've likely never considered. Here's the job description:

Title: Anchorite/anchoress. The name comes from the word you know: You'll be an anchor, holding the ship of the church in the right place, keeping it steady when storms arise.

Responsibilities: Here's the list of your responsibilities: Pray. That's it. Specifically, pray for the church.

Housing: Speaking of the church, that's where you'll live. More precisely, in a tiny room in the wall of the building. Don't worry—you'll have a window through which to watch the worship. And there'll likely be another window to the outside world, so passersby can ask you for prayer and spiritual direction.

Salary: None, of course, as you've renounced all worldly possessions.[1] You may be allowed to keep a cat for company.

Benefits: Following Christ, dying to self, and taking up your cross daily.

Orientation: You'll be installed as anchorite with a liturgy that is effectively a burial service—you'll be giving up your former life, dying to the world and all you knew of it beforehand. At the conclusion of the service, you'll be "buried alive," entombed by a wall built to enclose you in your anchor hold.

Duration: Lifelong. You won't ever leave this "tomb," except, perhaps, in rare emergencies. You'll spend all your days in your anchor hold. You'll wake, sleep, eat, and pray there for the rest of your life.

Opportunities for advancement: Death.

If this seems outlandish, you might be surprised to know anchorites and anchoresses were quite a thing in medieval England. One of the most famous—in our day, not in hers—was Julian of Norwich.

We don't know much about Julian—not even her birth name. When she became an anchoress she took the name of the church, St. Julian. We know she was born in 1342 and likely died in the mid-1410s. We also know she lived during very troubling, chaotic times.

DIVISION, DISSENT, DISEASE, DESPERATION

During Julian's life, the church was in disarray, with two claimants to the papacy, one residing in Avignon, France, and the other at the Vatican in Rome. Europe was bitterly divided between supporters of these rival papacies. In fact, Julian's own bishop led a crusade against the Avignon pope!

Unsurprisingly, given these problems, religious dissent was on the rise. Groups like the Lollards preached around the countryside, protesting church corruption and criticizing aspects of medieval theology. Lollards were executed as heretics only half a mile away from Julian's church.

Meanwhile, the Black Death ravaged Europe, reducing England's population almost by half. The plague came to Norwich twice during Julian's lifetime, once when she was six years old and again when she was nineteen. The devastating pandemic was widely interpreted as a terrible judgment from God.

What's more, there was economic unrest. High taxes and rising food prices led desperate peasants to riot and loot across England. Peasant uprisings—including in Julian's own town of Norwich—were violently put down by the authorities.

Division, dissent, disease, desperation. This is the world in which Julian decided to apply for the job description given above.

What would compel someone to abandon their former identity—to take a new name?

Why would they renounce ambition and devote the rest of their days to living in solitude?

In a world full of suffering, with so many needs, why choose to be entombed in a room where the only thing you could do is to pray?

The only way to make sense of Julian's choice is to conclude either that she was delusional or that she was *called*—that she had a vocation. (I suppose a third interpretation would be that Julian was a serious introvert—but she had to put up with lots of visitors at her window, so that theory falls apart.)

Vocation. Calling. Christians use these words a lot, generally to talk vaguely about our work and career. It's hard to know how the word could apply to Julian the anchoress, but also to a middle-class twentysomething with a university degree, or to a single mom of three, or to a recently immigrated family.

What does it mean for each of these people to have a vocation? To be called?

Does God call us to specific jobs, specific careers? Is our vocation just whatever career field we happen to be successful in?

DISENTANGLING: VOCATION, WORK, CAREER

Our culture prizes productivity. One of the first questions we ask upon meeting someone is "What do you do?" It's what someone does that defines them—more specifically, what they do for pay. Of course, work is good, including paid work. But we tend to make our occupation into our identity.

And in Christian circles, we often spiritualize this—we conflate our paid work with our purpose in life. When we talk about our "vocation," our calling, what we mean is our career.

This conflation is, at best, unhelpful. We need to expand our definition of vocation, to disentangle it from our cultural preoccupation with careers.

The best place to start is with Scripture. How does the Bible speak of vocation?

When you look for the language of vocation, of calling, in Scripture, you won't find much reference to jobs or careers. Instead, this language refers to the calling all Christians share: to follow Christ.

Paul loved to use the terms "call" and "calling." In his letters to the church in Rome and the church in Corinth, he addresses believers as "called ones," or "invited ones." This is our identity: We are those who have been called. More specifically, we've been called by God. We have been invited by God to share in His kingdom, to participate in His great purposes for the world. This calling changes everything. It's not just about what we get paid to do—it's a reorientation of our whole existence.

Vocation means that your identity, your purpose, your very life itself is found in Jesus Christ.

Already, this definition challenges several of our assumptions. First, your most important vocation is not unique to you. Your primary calling is shared with all members of Christ's church. The call is personal, but not individual; it's a call to be part of a people.

Another implication is that if you're confused about your vocation, if you find yourself wondering about God's call on your life, never fear. It's spelled out clearly in Scripture. Christ calls you just as He did His apostles: "Come, follow me" (Matt. 4:19).

Paul is happy to provide more details: Your calling is a gift from God (Rom. 11:29); your calling doesn't have anything to do with your natural abilities (1 Cor. 1:26); your calling is to holiness (2 Tim. 1:9); your calling is grounded in Christian hope (Eph. 1:18); your calling is something you strive to live up to (2 Thess. 1:11). If you want to know your vocation, it's right there in black and white. In short, it's to walk in the way of the cross.

A third implication is that career is at best secondary to vocation. More likely, it's even further down the list, ranked below things like our familial roles, our relationships with housemates and neighbors, our hobbies and unpaid work, our service toward others—these might be more central to our vocation than whatever we do to earn money. While your work is part of how you'll follow Christ, God's call is not reducible to your occupation.

This means that "discerning your vocation" isn't synonymous with picking a career field. Sure, you'll have to discern how *you* are meant to follow Christ. But first, we have to ask: What is included in our calling?

What are we called to as humans—humans who are created, fallen, and redeemed?

What, in other words, might we include in a theological account of vocation?

CREATED: MADE TO BE PRIESTS

In the opening chapter of Genesis, we read about the creation of humankind. It's immediately clear that Adam and Eve are called to a special role—to bridge, to go between, God and the rest of creation. On the one hand, we are given to creation on behalf of God. We are called to represent God, to be His "image and likeness," and to act on behalf of His authority in and for the rest of the world. On the other hand, we give creation back to God. We are called to recognize God's creation for what it is, to see it in all its wild colors and delightful diversity, and to give names to every aspect of it. Our naming makes creation an offering to God.

We might sum up this part of our human vocation as this—we're made to be priests. This might sound odd. But what a priest does is offer the world up to God. Our work is to see and name the world, and to offer it back up as a sacrifice.

And this is what we humans do—this kind of seeing and naming distinguishes us from the other animals. As Leon Kass and Robert Farrar Capon have taught us, humans do more than merely feed. It's possible for us to see the world as more than an object at hand for our own consumption. And this possibility is the basis for all human culture.

> When men and women live out their priestly callings, onions become French onion soup, marble becomes Michelangelo's *David* . . .

Vocation features centrally in W. H. Auden's *Horae Canonicae*, a sequence of poems based on the hours monks went to prayer. In one of them, "Sext," Auden celebrates our ancestors who took the "prodigious step" of culture-making—the first to take on a vocation:

There should be monuments, there should be odes,
to the nameless heroes who took it first,

to the first flaker of flints
who forgot his dinner,
the first collector of sea-shells
to remain celibate.[2]

The artist, the architect, the sculptor, the chef, the composer, the poet, the sea-shell collector: All attend, lovingly, to the world God has made, look long enough to see possibilities where others only glance at the surface, and through their hands or voices call forth something good, true, and beautiful.

When men and women live out their priestly callings, onions become French onion soup, marble becomes Michelangelo's *David*, grain and grape become bread and wine. Creation becomes more than it already was. Or, we might say even more boldly, creation is transformed into what it was always intended to become. It becomes a worthy offering; it becomes praise.

FALLEN: THE FUTILITY OF OUR VOCATION

Of course, the story continues after Genesis 2 and quickly takes a tragic turn. We are fallen. We've rebelled, turning away from what we were meant for, and this rebellion has infected every aspect of being human.

Instead of receiving our life as a gift from God, we want to live on our own terms. Instead of a loving attention that transforms creation into an offering, we treat things as objects that exist for our own use. Instead of our work participating in and reflecting God's goodness, truth, and beauty, we find it riddled with difficulty, pain, and meaninglessness.

Death means that all our work is marked by futility. Why plant a tree when you won't live long enough to enjoy its fruit? Why build a house when someone after you will sell it off to fund their irresponsible lifestyle? Why write a beautiful story when eventually it will be lost, or misunderstood, or conscripted into some cause you disagree with?

Anything you might do, anything you might build, will one day go the way of all things. "Vanity," writes the author of Ecclesiastes, "all is vanity."

But it's worse than that. Everything bound up in being human, everything that was meant for good, is bent inward, turned away from life and toward death. The result is not just meaninglessness, but idolatry, and injustice, and evil.

Auden's *Horae Canonicae* is set on Good Friday. And the poem I quoted from earlier, "Sext," occurs at the hour of noon. Auden observes that the very things that make us human—our work, our social life, our ability to deliberate, to craft, to pronounce—all these make possible the crucifixion. They all culminate in a moment just after noon on a hill outside Jerusalem. What do we do with God's gifts? With our ingenuity, our reason, our creativity? We kill God.

In the next poem in the sequence, set in the heat of the afternoon, Auden reflects on how everything looks different after the cross.

> Under the mock chase and mock capture,
> The racing and tussling and splashing,
> The panting and the laughter,
> Be listening for the cry and stillness
> To follow after: wherever
> The sun shines, brooks run, books are written,
> There will also be this death.[3]

After the cross, even the most innocent pastimes, even our play, seem sinister. We caught our victim and killed him.

When we look at the cross, we see something awful: We see the truth about ourselves. The worst thing that could ever happen has happened, and we did it. And, throughout history, we've done it again and again: From Cain and Abel to world wars, from tribal spats to nuclear weapons, we've used the gifts of being human to destroy.

In this fallen world, our vocation is futile. It not only ends in death but actively brings about death. At best, it's meaningless; at worst, it's crucifying Christ.

REDEEMED: FOLLOWING CHRIST TO THE CROSS

The good news is that while the cross is the worst thing we've ever done, it's also the means by which God saves us.

And the cross transforms our human vocation. Or, we might say, it *becomes* our human vocation.

I think we tend to look at the cross and see it as revealing something about God—it shows us the great extent of God's mercy and love. And that's 100 percent correct. But everything Jesus does, including the cross, also shows us something true about being human.

In the early fifth century, the church was troubled by a teaching called "Nestorianism," which wanted to clearly differentiate between the divine Son of God and the human Jesus. Nestorius was concerned to distinguish what things Jesus Christ did as *God*, and what things He did as *man*. The church came to reject this teaching, in large part because of Cyril, bishop of Alexandria.

Cyril insisted, against Nestorius, that we can't split Jesus in two. Jesus isn't 50/50—He's not half human and half divine. Rather, Christ's two natures are perfectly united in one person, and everything Christ does, He does as that one person. In other words, Jesus Christ not only shows us what God is like, He also perfectly shows us humanity. All that we were made

> **What does true humanity look like? Self-giving instead of self-preservation, forgiveness instead of vengeance.**

for, all that God had in mind, is completed by the incarnate Son of God, the new Adam.

The letter to the Hebrews puts it this way: Christ shares in our humanity—"like his brethren in every respect"—and fulfills the creation mandate (Heb. 2:17); He is our "great high priest" who knows all of our weakness and frailty (Heb. 4:14); He has offered up His very life, making "for all time a single sacrifice for sins" (Heb. 10:12). Jesus fulfills our human vocation.

This means that in the cross, we see what true humanity looks like. What does it mean to be human? To be self-giving instead of self-preserving, forgiving instead of seeking vengeance. Sacrificial love.

So far, so good. But Cyril has more to say about the unity of Christ. What Christ accomplished on the cross, and in His resurrection, He did in His humanity, not *just* because He was divine. Before Christ, death was more powerful than humanity. But Christ conquered death *as man*: "The one that overcame death was one of us," Cyril writes. "If he conquered as God, to us it is nothing; but if he conquered as man we conquered in Him."[4] For Cyril, Christ's victory forever changed what it means to be human—it opened up entirely new possibilities.

If you want to be fully human, there's just one way to do it: "Take up your cross and follow me." As Dietrich Bonhoeffer put it, only a few years before he met his death in a Nazi prison camp, "When Christ calls a man, he bids him come and die."[5]

The way of the cross is the true human vocation. Or, we might say, the way of life is through death. Or, as Someone else once said, you can only save your life by losing it.

What are we supposed to do with this?

What kind of life advice book, what kind of career counseling session, starts with "come and die"?

How are we to translate Christ's crucifixion to the cross we're supposed to pick up? How can we possibly imitate the Son of God, the only sinless man?

The apostle Paul instructed the church in Corinth, "Be imitators of me, as I am of Christ" (1 Cor. 11:1). We learn to walk in the way of the cross by following those who have already followed Christ down that path.

SO GREAT A CLOUD OF WITNESSES

Why does Paul tell his readers, "Imitate me"? Why not just skip over Paul and go straight to imitating Christ? Wouldn't it be better if we exclusively looked to Christ for example and inspiration, and never to anyone else?

The letter to the Hebrews is once again instructive. After celebrating the uniqueness and sufficiency of Jesus, the author draws our attention to a long list of saints in chapter 11, praising their valor, faith, and martyrdoms. We're instructed in chapter 12 to run the race with these saints in view. We will "run with perseverance" as we're cheered on by this "great cloud of witnesses," who watch from the heavenly grandstand, so to speak. We draw inspiration from them, and they root us on.

We might balk at the notion that the saints take part in our lives here and now. Aren't they dead, after all? Well, kind of? The saints might be dead, but they haven't ceased to exist. "He is not God of the dead, but of the living," we are reminded in Matthew 22:32.

As we proclaim in the creed, we participate in "the communion of the saints." By virtue of belonging to Christ's body, and sharing the same Holy Spirit, we are one in union with all of God's people. And this communion isn't severed by death. Christ's triumph over death means there is no unbridgeable divide between the church militant (on earth) and the church triumphant (in heaven). This is why, in the book of Revelation, we see martyred saints gathered around the throne of God, praying about what the church is going through on earth.

Of course, Christians disagree about what exactly is entailed by the communion of the saints. But, with the book of Hebrews, we should at least be inspired by those who have gone before us. We see this in the earliest records of Christian worship and prayer. The *Didache* instructs, "And you shall seek out day by day the faces of the saints, in order that you may rest upon their words."

Martyrs, especially, played a big role in the life of the early church. Christians wrote and distributed stories like the "Martyrdom of Felicity and Perpetua," written around AD 202. They noted the dates of martyrs' deaths, annually honoring the anniversary of each triumph. Their bodies also mattered. Christians carefully gathered and buried the remains of Ignatius of Antioch (martyred in AD 107) and Polycarp (martyred in AD 156) and others. The early church held these figures near and dear.

Circling back to our bigger question: How might these saints help us better understand our vocation?

Each of us has a vision of the good life, a set of stories that tell us what to expect and hope for out of life. This vision has been shaped by all sorts of things, from proverbs passed down from our family ("God helps those who help themselves") to national origin stories ("life, liberty, and the pursuit of happiness") to the cultural scripts we sing ("It's my life, and it's now or never / I ain't gonna live forever"). These shape our desires and dictate our hopes.

Stories of the saints offer a different image. And "different" is the right word: The saints are anything but boring! "How monotonously alike all the great tyrants and conquerors have been," C. S. Lewis put it, "how gloriously different are the saints."[6] From hermits who battled demons in the desert, to wise abbesses whose courage thwarted robbers, to contemplatives whose marveling at creation produced scientific insights, to homeless vagabonds who befriended animals, to scholars who preserved classical learning, to pregnant mothers who stared death in the face and didn't flinch—there are endless ways to take up your cross. In all their wild and wooly diversity, the saints help us reimagine what it looks like to respond to the call of Christ.

The saints also highlight a gap in our usual talk about vocation: suffering. My wife has helped me see this. As a spiritual director and a professional life coach, Paige has had hundreds of conversations with young adults about their vocational questions. She's noticed that we're prone to think of suffering as a sign that we've gotten our vocation wrong. This makes it even more painful when life inevitably takes a hard turn.

As Paige pointed out, we should *expect* our vocation to include suffering. Suffering is not an indicator that God is far away—it is not an indicator that you missed the "right" path. And the opposite is true too. If you're flying high, that doesn't mean that you've "found it." This is a truth that the saints illustrate in vivid color, because their lives are usually full of suffering.

If we don't look to the saints, we'll still have a vision of the good life. We'll have stories and heroes that tell us which way to aim our lives. They just might not be the best and truest ones. The saints help us to imagine how transformative God's grace is, what new humanity is capable of, and how, "walking in the way of the Cross, we may find it none other than the way of life and peace."

Julian of Norwich didn't live what most people would recognize as "the good life." Her life was marked by pain, illness, and solitude.

She lived and died in relative obscurity—her *Revelations of Divine Love* were read by almost no one until the late 1600s, and only widely read in the last hundred years or so. As I already mentioned, we don't even know her birth name.

Like all of us, Julian's life was one long, slow death (only, she was entombed for more of hers than we tend to be).

But Julian had been transformed by the love of Christ. She was so transfixed by divine love that she could marvel at the simple, fragile beauty of a hazelnut, could long to experience Christ's suffering in her own body, could write what God had revealed: That in the end, "all shall be well, and all shall be well, and all manner of things shall be well."

"There is only one tragedy in the end," the French novelist Léon Bloy writes. "Not to have been a saint."[7]

O God, whose Son Jesus Christ is the Good
Shepherd of your people:
Grant that, when we hear his voice, we may
know him who calls us each by name,
and follow where he leads; who, with you
and the Holy Spirit, lives and reigns,
one God, for ever and ever. Amen.

Collect for Good Shepherd Sunday,
the *Book of Common Prayer*

11

Hearing His Voice
The Lifelong Project of Discernment

The first year of Brazos Fellows held a memorable conversation. One of the fellows started the year with a clear sense of what she was going to do with her life. After acing a robust four-year liberal arts degree and thriving in a well-placed internship, she was going to knock fellows out of the park, go to DC, and change the world.

Then she started to have doubts. After months of prayer and study—reading Julian of Norwich, Augustine, Teresa of Avila, W. H. Auden, and others—she slowly came to question all her reasons for taking this path. She realized her career plans hinged on expectations others had put on her, on the pressure she felt to "make a big difference." Her plans started to crumble like a house of cards. With chagrin, she told me this program, designed to support emerging adults in their vocational discernment, had an unexpected result: "Now I'm more confused about what I should do than ever!"

We joked that her story made for *great* marketing copy. Picture the ads: "Come do Brazos Fellows and become more confused." Or, as a later cohort of fellows suggested, "Brazos Fellows: Not useful."

Joking aside, her confusion—while not the goal—was progress. It was far better that she ask those hard questions and reconsider her own assumptions at twenty-two years old than to wake up in her forties and realize she'd never seriously considered her path. Far better to wrestle at the outset than to build a life based on unquestioned certainties.

You'll remember that my experience as a college senior was on the other end of the spectrum. Unlike this Brazos Fellow, I had no idea coming out of college what I should do with my life. All of my friends had answers to the dreaded question, "What's next after graduation?" Not I. It took more than a few years after graduating to find a path I felt confident taking. Even though I was supported by my community during those years, I still felt a sense of failure. I didn't know where I was going. I wasn't changing the world. Somewhere along the way I'd dropped the ball, or driven past my exit, or missed my boat coming in.

I couldn't know then what I know now. But, if I could time travel, I'd tell my early-twenties self a few things. First, I'd suggest living by a common rule with my friends. And then I'd say what I tell college seniors all the time: Not only is it *not bad* you're unsure what's next, it's actually *better*. That's right. Against career counselors everywhere, I boldly take my stand: It might be good you don't know what you're doing next.

I'm overstating it to make a point. But indulge me for a bit: Let's see how strong a case we can make for the goodness of not knowing.

THE CASE FOR NOT KNOWING WHAT'S NEXT

First, "what you're doing next" is very likely to be impermanent. If you're an American in your twenties, you're four times more likely to change jobs than your parents were. This is the reality of the world we live in, and the trend is only increasing: In 2022, 50 million

Americans quit their jobs;[1] in the same year, one out of three Americans between the ages of twenty-five and forty-four reported that they were considering switching to a different career field.[2] Our grandparents tended to be lifers, working for one company and retiring with a pension; our parents changed jobs a few times; you'll be odd among your generation if you work for the same company for a decade.

I think of friends whose lives took unexpected turns. They read a book, audited a class for fun, grabbed a coffee with that kind man, suddenly lost a parent or a spouse, were told something profound by a mentor, had a baby, went with a friend to their church's vigil—and life took an unexpected turn. Now, their lives look entirely different than planned. This is, of course, how life always goes, for all of us, at some point or another.

Paige and I could never have guessed even ten years ago that we'd be living in Waco and directing Brazos Fellows. Even a few years ago, we weren't sure where this work was going. Discernment, decision-making, choosing between occupational paths—this is work that hasn't stopped through our thirties. Other close friends, and plenty of alumni among the Brazos Fellows, would say the same thing.

> Life won't meet your expectations. Your path won't be perfectly straight. Surprises await, both good and bad.

In this light, knowing that you don't "know what's next" looks rather like wisdom. Life won't meet your expectations. Your path won't be perfectly straight. Surprises await, both good and bad. Thinking you know might be a deadly presumption. You know who doesn't know what's next? The birds of the air, Jesus tells us, the flowers of the field. What if our not knowing, instead of being a source of anxiety (which cannot "add one cubit to our span of life"), could become a trusting open-handedness?

Second, not knowing "what you're doing next" allows you to focus on more important things. Who you're becoming is exponentially more important than what job you're doing. That's why this book isn't titled *Ten Easy Steps for Figuring Everything Out!* or *Three Keys to Absolutely Crushing Your Calling.* This book is about *becoming*, becoming people whose lives are structured by prayer, community, and study.

As it turns out, the central practices of this way of life (community, prayer, study, Sabbath) aren't tools we use to figure out our vocation; they *are* the vocation.

> Career, money, profession tend to take up all the space we let them. Unchecked, they will *always* claim ultimate importance.

So if you and your friends have committed to this common rule, it might be more accurate to say that you *do* know what you're doing next, at least when it comes to what's most important. It's just that you don't know as many details about peripheral things, like your career.

Let me be clear: I'm not trying to demean anyone's occupation, or pretend that earning money doesn't matter. Saying something is *more* important doesn't mean the other thing is *unimportant*. We're talking better and best, not good and bad.

But career, money, profession all tend to dominate. They take up all the space we let them. Unchecked, they will *always* claim ultimate importance, demand our greatest attention, and, ultimately, become our identity. If we succeed, we will no longer depend on God.

In Luke 12, Jesus tells a parable of a rich man who said to himself, "'Soul, you have ample goods laid up for many years; take your ease, eat, drink, be merry.' But God said to him, 'Fool! This night your soul is required of you; and the things you have prepared, whose will they be?' So is he who lays up treasure for himself, and is not rich toward God" (Luke 12:19–21).

A bit of agnosticism about the future, a bit of holy indifference, a bit of impracticality, might save us.

Third, not knowing "what you're doing next" means you can actively wait. It's not bad to make goals. Thinking ahead, imagining what's next, making a plan, trying to pull it off—these are things we need to do. And none of these are incompatible with waiting.

Waiting doesn't mean passivity. The kind of waiting we're talking about, a waiting that seeks discernment, isn't something you're stuck in but something you choose. It's *willful*. It's attentive. And, in fact, it's hard work. It's the kind of struggle that comes with the question, What is the Lord asking of me? To ask this, genuinely, and to listen, patiently, is quite difficult.

Wisdom is required here. Not making plans, standing still and not stepping out onto the path, might be imprudent or even sinful. It might be a way of evading responsibility or indulging in apathy. Some people take a "gap year" to pray, seek counsel, and open themselves to God's leading; others take it to extend the college lifestyle for another year (or two, or three).

But waiting can also be a way of focusing on the present. My friend Ben puts it this way: "We all have vocations right now, and I would argue that practicing our present vocations is actually more important than deciding on our future vocations."[3] Or as a spiritual director in the Ignatian tradition puts it, "Discernment is an active prayer process in which we look for where God is working in me, in others, and in the world, and we seek to do what God is doing with Him."[4] Instead of starting with me and my future—"What should I be up to next?"—what if I started with the question, "What is God up to now?" Asking the second question might be the best way to find an answer to the first.

Discernment isn't something we figure out before getting started. Often, we find answers while on the road. We wake into a new day, walk out our front door, and decide which way to turn. We make plans, and we pursue them. We ask God to guide our steps—and we keep asking while we're taking them.

Fourth, and finally, God's not in a rush for you to figure out "what to do next." You may feel compelled to get your career going. Sometimes, this sense of urgency comes from well-meaning parents (or future in-laws). Or, this urgency might come from within. Aware of our privilege, of all we've been given, of those who poured into us, we feel compelled to start giving back. In a world with so much spiritual and physical need, how could we justify delay?

Sometime in the middle of the first century AD, an ardent Jew was traveling from Jerusalem to Damascus when he got knocked off his horse. We've all heard how Saul, zealous persecutor of the church, was converted to Paul the apostle. But one detail of the story we miss is what happened in between. After his conversion, it would be fourteen years before Paul went on his first missionary journey. For a good portion of this time he was in the Arabian desert, studying, praying, and being transformed.[5]

There's a certain absurdity to this. Paul will be the greatest church planter, the most important missionary, in the history of Christianity. And his ministry will be relatively short—around fifteen years or so—before his martyrdom. Why take so long to get started? Why didn't God get him going right after Damascus? Wouldn't twice as many years as a missionary make more sense? Why "waste" half of his post-conversion life?

Apparently, it took time to turn Saul into Paul. The one who was so sure of his own righteousness, who persecuted Christ, needed to spend years in the wilderness becoming someone God could use. What looks to us like a waste of time was the most important work Paul could do.

If Paul's life looks inefficient, consider Jesus' life. God becomes man, enters a world full of sin and suffering, and then, for thirty years, toils away as an anonymous carpenter in a small town. Think of all the good Jesus could have done if He'd launched His career in His early twenties! Think of all the sick who went unhealed, the hungry who went unfed, the people who never heard the kingdom proclaimed.

Jesus' timing makes no sense from our human perspective. We're constrained by time, and obsessed with efficiency and results.

Unlike us, God isn't in a rush. God has all the time in the world—literally.

Maybe our sense of urgency doesn't come from the Lord. Maybe being in a rush is just as likely to be unfaithful as it is to be faithful.

What would it look like to approach discernment with the awareness that God isn't in a hurry with us? That we might not be behind?

DISCERNMENT: A WAY OF LIFE

Whether you're totally unsure what to do, preparing for something specific, or already have meaningful work, it still remains that you need to discern. You need to continue listening. The Christian life isn't something we figure out by the time we're twenty-one and then coast from there. In fact, I'm not sure it's something we "figure out" at all. Sometimes we use the word "discernment" to mean something more like "deciphering." It's as if God has a secret plan for my life, and for some reason, He's hiding it from me. My job is to decode what that plan is and then get on with it.

I don't think that's right. God doesn't deliberately obscure from us what we need to know. Again and again in Scripture, God tells us what our vocation is. We need to discern what it means for *me* to hear and respond to that call, but that's vastly different than solving a riddle or cracking a code.

And it's not a onetime thing. Discernment is a mode of being, an ongoing process in which we ask the question again and again, seeking to remain open to an unexpected answer. Perhaps you'll be discerning your vocation right up until the day you die.

And this is one reason that Lent is so helpful.

I'm writing this chapter during Lent. Just a few days ago, I knelt in my Anglican church, and my priest smeared ashes in the shape of the cross on my forehead. Ash Wednesday kicked off a season when we remember our need for ongoing repentance. Every year, we recognize that we're not finished in the spiritual life. The work of sanctification isn't complete. So we take forty days to pay greater attention than usual to our neediness, our sin, our mortality, our coming death. From dust we came, and to dust we will return.

Since we're only a few days in, I can report that Lent is going great. I've made my confession, I'm on top of my Lenten fast. So far, so good. But check back with me in a week or two. During these forty days, I'll struggle and weaken, and by the time we're about to enter Holy Week, which starts with Palm Sunday and ends with Easter Sunday, I'll once again feel like I've failed at Lent.

In a sense, that's okay. As my friend Jonathan recently reminded me, fasting isn't about me accomplishing something spiritually, but about opening up space for *God* to accomplish something within me. Lent strips away our pretensions; it undermines our sense that we're doing pretty well overall. When we let go of presumption, embracing our frailty and weakness, we open ourselves up to God's transformation.

In other words, Lent invites us to reevaluate our life, to revisit our calling—to create space, through fasting, prayer, and silence, for God to speak.

While Lent is a great time to focus on this, it's something we should practice all the time. Discernment is a way of life—a life of prayer, self-examination, and confession. Daniel Wright, a priest at an Orthodox church in Waco, calls this "existential repentance." This form of repentance takes place when we regularly ask God questions like these:

In light of my coming death, how should I live?
What, God, do You call me to?
Where are You inviting me to meet with You?
From what do I need to turn away?
How might I turn back to You?

Asking these questions, making them part of your life, is hard work. It's not easy to sit with these questions. It's uncomfortable to really mean them. It's tough to find time for this kind of silence, prayer, and reflection. So what do we do?

THE EXAMINED LIFE

I struggle to attend to my inner life. I find it difficult to name what's going on inside, and even more difficult to notice patterns and trajectories. If someone asks me how things are going in my Christian walk, I fumble around before listing things I wish I were doing better.

Part of the problem is my personality, but another part is just how distracting life is. If only I lived before social media or TV, then I'd be able to really pay attention. If only I had more opportunity for silence and stillness, then we could really sit with big questions.

One of the great things about studying church history is realizing that there's nothing new—including being distracted in our spiritual life. In the fifth century, John Cassian complained about how easy it was to be distracted during prayer. "The mind, as it is always light and wandering, is distracted even in time of service by all sorts of things," he writes, "as if it were intoxicated." It turns out, we don't need flickering screens to distract us. Our own wandering minds are quite capable on their own.

Thankfully, the church has accumulated much wisdom on how to win the battle. Cassian, for example, suggests the value of memorization and repetition: Recite the same psalm, again and again, to teach your mind focus.[6] Over the centuries, Christians have found various ways to stay focused, such as slow, meditative reading of Scripture, a practice called *lectio divina*.[7]

Another helpful practice is one we've already introduced: the Ignatian Examen. The Examen invites you to reflect on the movement of your heart that day. When did you draw close to God? When did you feel yourself moving away from God? When you pray the Examen day after day, attending to these "consolations" and "desolations," you become more aware of what's going on in your spiritual life.

Recently, my spiritual director, Michael, an Anglican priest, impressed on me the significance of the first question God asks us: "Where are you?" We easily wander from God. We might not even be aware that we've wandered. Yet God doesn't remain aloof or far away; He comes looking for us, and He speaks to us. "Where are you?"

Praying the Examen can be a way of taking seriously God's question. In five or ten minutes a day, you can hear this question anew, and prayerfully attend to your consolations and desolations. Be sure to take notes. Over time, you'll notice more, remembering that the point of the Examen is not to keep some sort of spiritual scorecard. Rather, the aim is to grow in discernment: to learn to recognize the voice of your Lord.

DON'T GO IT ALONE: RECEIVING SPIRITUAL DIRECTION

As good as the Examen is, Ignatius never intended this kind of prayerful self-examination to be done in isolation. Most of us aren't great at introspection. Left to our own devices, we can only get so far. We easily self-justify, rationalizing all of our decisions and commitments, and thus falling into pride; or, we fall prey to scrupulosity, beating ourselves up and despairing of God's goodness. Whether you tend toward the sin of presumption or the sin of despair, you need someone else to attend to your spiritual life alongside you.

Spiritual direction is one way not to go it alone. Simply, a spiritual director is someone who sits with you, prays with you, and helps you notice what God is up to in your life. They ask questions of you, and of the Lord, and listen. They help you focus your attention, to see, to hear. In this sense, they are like a physical therapist but for your spiritual senses: helping you slowly build "muscle," learn movement, that will allow you to better know and receive God's love.

If you don't know anyone who practices spiritual direction, a pastor, or a wise, more mature Christian might play a similar role in your life. Over time, a good mentor or spiritual director will be able to discern, and help you discern, what God is up to. Sometimes, this will involve a word of advice, or caution. Sometimes it'll provide a space to sort through a specific question or decision you have. And, sometimes, it might involve you recognizing sin that you didn't see before.

Depending on your church tradition, a spiritual director might also be trained to hear your confession. For many Protestants, confessing sins to a priest sounds strange or wrong—as if we won't be forgiven unless we do something extra. But, in my tradition, the Anglican church, the point of confession isn't to wipe away the guilt of your sin—that's been taken care of by Christ's work on the cross.

Here's the thing: The consequences of sin include more than just guilt. Our sin also mars relationships. It hurts others; it hurts *us*. So while we need forgiveness for our sins, we also need healing. In his epistle, James instructs us to "confess your sins to one another, and pray for one another, that you may be healed" (5:16).

What does this look like? In preparing to make my confession, I pray and ask the Holy Spirit to show me my sin and, reflecting on God's commandments, list all of the ways I've fallen short. Then I go to a priest or minister and read my list out loud. These are the bad things I've done, said, and thought. These are the ways I've failed to love God and neighbor. I don't hide or cover my sin by using euphemisms: These things are wrong, I say, and I did them.

In response, I don't hear condemnation or disgust but rather God's forgiveness and acceptance. Often, I receive words of counsel and instruction. And the result? Sin is robbed of its power. We let the light in, and the darkness flees. Speaking for myself, I've experienced profound healing through confession. That's why I encourage you, if you're in a church tradition that offers confession, to take advantage of this gift.

"I'm more confused," said our Brazos Fellow that first year. As she learned, slowing down to do the work of discernment—to pray, confess, listen, study, examine yourself—comes with a risk. You might end up discerning that the future path you envisioned isn't actually the way you should go. Slowing down might prove to be rather impractical. Admittedly, this chapter isn't very practically minded. If you were looking for some handy-dandy strategies for building your career, you might be disappointed to get advice like "pray" and "tell someone about the bad stuff you've done."

But there are plenty of other books out there on growing up, finding mentors, and strategically starting your career. And, if you're like me and come out of college not knowing what to do with your life, or if you're like our first-year Brazos Fellow and find your plan falling apart, take heart. Sometimes, the next step starts with being knocked off your horse. In whatever uncertainty or confusion you find yourself, you've been given a gift: the chance to pause, pray, and discern. And then to get back on the road, and do more of the same.

Almighty God, who after the creation of the
world rested from all your works
and sanctified a day of rest for all your
creatures: Grant that we,
putting away all earthly anxieties, may
be duly prepared for the service of your
sanctuary,
and that our rest here upon earth may be a
preparation for the eternal rest promised to
your people in heaven; through Jesus Christ
our Lord. Amen.

Collect for Sabbath Rest,
the *Book of Common Prayer*

12

Practicing Sabbath

I first encountered the idea of Sabbath when I was around ten years old. I told an elderly volunteer in my dad's ministry that the day before my family had gone out for ice cream. She raised her eyebrows in judgment: Ice cream on a Sunday? On the Sabbath? Tsk, tsk.

Maybe that's what you think of when you hear "Sabbath." Long-faced Puritans banning fun and games, or "blue laws" that limit alcohol sales after sundown on Saturday, or a list of things you should feel guilty for doing on Sundays. Joyless sanctimony at best and legalism at worst.

Several years after college, Paige and I encountered a different vision of Sabbath in a summer class at Regent College with theologian Marva Dawn. Marva taught us that keeping the Sabbath was not dreary or burdensome but life-giving. Sabbath, she told us, invites us to participate in God's rest.

This sounded too good to be true—especially to two people driven by endless productivity. In our early twenties, Paige and I had a compulsive need to prove our value by working our hardest, only stopping when we crashed from exhaustion or illness. To our ears, Sabbath both sounded incredibly inviting and *totally impossible.*

Near the end of our class, Paige asked Marva, "But what if I'm not ready when Sabbath comes around? What if I haven't done enough?" With a compassionate smile, Marva said it like it was: "You've missed the point entirely!" Sabbath, she explained, is never merited. It always comes to us as an undeserved gift, regardless of what we've done or left undone. Sabbath breaks in whether we're "ready" for it or not.

That conversation, fifteen years ago, set our lives on a different trajectory. Practicing Sabbath over the years has transformed our life together. Marva was right: Sabbath is a gift.

What does the gift of Sabbath entail?

What might it mean to accept this gift?

And what might the practice of Sabbath have to do with discerning our vocation?

THE GIFT OF SABBATH

It's curious that at the beginning of the story of Scripture we find God resting. Genesis 2 begins, "God blessed the seventh day and hallowed it, because on it God rested from all his work which he had done in creation."

Why in the world does God rest? For us creatures, rest is necessary. We must cease from working in order to get back to producing. We rest because of our finitude, our limitations. None of this is true of God. Instead of God's rest being a means to greater productivity, His work is oriented toward His rest. He creates so that creation can share in His eternal delight.

Put another way, the point of God's creation is to be at rest with us. At the end of the seven days, God comes to rest, to indwell, the temple He has made. Creation is the story of God making a home where He will dwell with us.

Our beginning tells us something about our future. Augustine taught that God's rest in the beginning points to the end of time.

What we're created for, where we're eventually headed, is resting in the presence of God. "We shall ourselves be the seventh day, when we shall be filled and replenished with God's blessing and sanctification," Augustine writes. "There shall we be still, and know that He is God."[1]

In between the first act (creation) and the final act (the eschaton), Sabbath is central to the middle act (redemption). For Israel, Sabbath was all about remembering their redemption: "You shall remember that you were a servant in the land of Egypt, and the LORD your God brought you out thence with a mighty hand and an outstretched arm; therefore the LORD your God commanded you to keep the sabbath day" (Deut. 5:15). By observing the Sabbath, Israel recalled and celebrated how the Lord had delivered them from slavery and bondage.

Sabbath rest isn't a matter of optimization. We don't take off one day out of seven to "recharge" so we can get back to greater productivity. Rather, we rest because we're made to be with God. We rest because we've been delivered from captivity to death and sin. And we rest because Sabbath is where we're headed—it's our final purpose, our *telos*.

If this is the theological meaning of Sabbath, how do we live it out practically?

In her book *Keeping the Sabbath Wholly*, Marva Dawn offers four Sabbath practices: ceasing, resting, embracing, and feasting:

Ceasing: We cease from work, including all the ordinary tasks that "need" to be done. How can we justify this unproductivity? Remembering that our life does not depend on us. Our very existence, and all we need, has been given to us as a gift. Why do we cease? Because we remember we are not God, and the world will keep turning without our help.

Resting: We enter intentionally into rest. How is rest more than ceasing? Unlike much of our downtime, true rest is attentive, engaged, perhaps even active. We might even call it contemplative. Why do we rest? Because before we did anything at all, God called His creation "very good."

Embracing: We embrace God and embrace each other. Sabbath is not "me time." It's not about escaping from others so we can recharge. Instead, unencumbered by to-do lists and crammed schedules, we are free to be present with others. Why do we embrace? Because we were made to be in relationship; we were meant to embrace and be embraced in love.

Feasting: We "taste and see that the Lord is good" (Ps. 34:8). First and foremost, we do this in worship, feasting on word and sacrament. And then we feast on all other kinds of goodness: music, poetry, stories, nature, excellent company, good food and drink. Why do we feast? Because, in feasting, we get a foretaste of that heavenly banquet that our divine Bridegroom is preparing for us.

As this last practice makes most clear, all of our Sabbath-keeping centers around a main event: gathering as the church.

LET US KEEP THE FEAST: THE RADICAL IDEA OF GOING TO CHURCH

A decade or so ago, a spate of books came out urging American Christians to be "radical"—not to settle for conventional, ordinary faith, but to go all-in. This is a good exhortation, as far as it goes. But it's left me wanting to write a very short book titled *Radical Christianity*, the entire body of which would be two sentences: Want to be radical? Go to church.

I'm not kidding. Going to church puts you in a shrinking minority of self-proclaimed Christians. Fewer people who identify as "evangelical" attend—let alone actively participate in—their local church. American denominations already saw declining attendance before Covid; in the wake of the pandemic, almost all remain significantly below their 2019 attendance numbers.

Some blame for this trend should be put on what theologian J. I. Packer called the "stunted ecclesiology" of evangelicalism. This deficiency is summed up in what a college student once told me: "Church is good, but it's not a requirement. It's not essential to my walk with the Lord." I've already critiqued this all-too-common view. You can't separate your relationship with Christ from belonging to His body.

But I think there's another misconception that feeds this stunted ecclesiology: the notion that Sunday offers an escape from everyday life—that we go to worship once a week to get filled up before going back to the "real world." Alexander Schmemann calls this the "heresy of secularism." Secularism asserts that the meaning of this world can be found within itself. To help us get by, this heresy goes, we turn to religion, which has nothing to do with this life. In other words, what we do on Sundays simply helps us to cope in a secular world by promising our eventual escape from it.

If that's what American Christians think "going to church" is about, no wonder that fewer and fewer bother. If you're looking for something to help you get through the week, there are far better "solutions" than a ninety-minute inspirational service. Better to fill up your Sunday morning with youth sports, exercise, boozy brunches, or sleeping in.

Schmemann continues: Instead of offering escape from this world, the church's worship is about participating in the truth about *all of life*. When we celebrate Communion, we partake in what's really real. Our Sunday worship "is the entrance of the Church into the joy of its Lord. And, to enter into that joy, so as to be a witness to it in the world, is indeed the very calling of the Church."[2]

To be sure, church doesn't always feel joyful. Sometimes church can feel difficult, dull, or socially challenging. Sometimes we'd rather sleep in. But Sabbath isn't about us feeling happy or peaceful or fulfilled. It's not about a feeling at all.

When we wake up on a Sunday morning, get out the door, and find our way to our seat, we're not just ticking the "religious" box on our weekly to-do list. We're not gathering to optimize our best life now, or to be slightly more decent to each other. We come together, Schmemann writes, "to be transformed into the Church of God."[3]

In other words, we gather on Sunday mornings to become who we are. We were made for worship, to share in the delight and joy of God's love. This is what's most true about us—it's our purpose, our destiny. In short, we go to church because we are *called*. To be the church is our vocation.

LEARNING TO ATTEND: SABBATH PRACTICES

So you've started your Sabbath off right: You've gone to church. Radical! What about the rest of the day? What else might Sabbath include?

I suspect that out of Marva's four practices, the hardest one is rest. At least for me, resting is the practice I need the most reeducation on.

Much of what we do when we think we're resting is entirely passive, what we call "vegging" or "crashing" or "unwinding." Almost always, this takes the form of mindless electronic entertainment, and we feel justified in this because we feel so exhausted. Ironically, these weak imitations of rest usually leave us more tired. (Again, listen to Matt Anderson: Quit Netflix.)

"Vegging" results from life in what twentieth-century German philosopher Josef Pieper calls a culture of "total work." The world of total work is one where the meaning and significance of our lives is measured by our productivity (and our consumption). In this world, even our "rest" becomes about acquiring and consuming.

Pieper diagnoses "total work" as a moral and spiritual illness. The remedy? A recovery of "leisure," which means "an attitude of the mind, a condition of the soul," in which we are ready to receive reality. Leisure is "the capacity for steeping oneself in the whole of creation."[4] Writing in the 1940s, Pieper feared that modern society was losing something essentially human: the ability to receive a gift. In other words, we need to relearn *receptivity*.

Receptivity explains the nuance between ceasing and resting. True rest isn't passive—it doesn't involve turning off your mind. Instead, true rest is engaged and intentional; it's more likely to involve stillness than screens. It doesn't leave you emptier; it fills you up. It doesn't get you ready to get back to the real world; it is, in itself, helping you enter more deeply into reality. In short, this kind of rest involves *attending*.

What are some ways of attentively resting?

PRACTICE SILENCE. As theologian Gordon Smith puts it, "To discern well we must pay attention: we need to observe and listen, noting what is happening around us and within us and attending to what others are saying."[5] But how can we pay attention when we live with almost constant noise? We spend much of the day talking, texting, swiping, commenting, and even multitask our noise, listening to music while watching a show, or reading with the TV on.

What do we miss? What's underneath all this noise?

What might we hear if we stopped to listen?

Consider taking on silence as a Sabbath practice. Devote a single hour to silence, ideally outdoors, without any screens. A slow, leisurely walk is particularly conducive to listening—your body in motion can help your mind be still. (I recently learned from a friend about a TikTok fad called "silent walking" in which people just walk around without earbuds in. You know something is deeply wrong when we have to rediscover the goodness of walking in silence.)

Silence, according to Pieper, is more than an absence of speech. It is a "receptive attitude of mind," a serenity in which we are open to letting things happen.[6] Try to enter your time of silence without any agenda. Ask the Lord to speak, then listen and wait. Perhaps hold off on writing or journaling at first. Reserve time at the end to capture some of the thoughts, questions, and prayers that have come up.

Finally, silence and stillness should sometimes be solitary practices—but not always. Why not spend a quiet hour in the company of good friends? To simply be present and still, to listen together?

CONTEMPLATE BEAUTY. Aesthetic delight is a noninstrumental good. Delighting in beauty is good in itself, not simply as a means to another end. How might we give more time to this intrinsic goodness? How do we practice patient attention to beauty?

Go for a nature walk. Delight in the beautiful diversity of the world God has called "very good." Learn to notice, to identify what you see and hear. How many species of animals do you encounter? How many bugs? How many strains of birdsong—and can you identify any? What about trees? Become a student of creation, and learn, as the poet Gerard Manley Hopkins did, to give glory to God "for skies of couple-colour as a brinded cow; / For rose-moles all in stipple upon trout that swim; / Fresh-firecoal chestnut-falls; finches' wings . . ."[7]

Speaking of Hopkins: *Read a poem, then reread it, then reread it again*. For the uninitiated, among whom I am numbered, poetry can intimidate. But difficulty doesn't mean there's a problem with you, or with the poetry. Great poems reward repeated attention. Give yourself to a Hopkins or a George Herbert or a Christina Rossetti poem. Even better, memorize one, and recite it as a Sabbath practice (perhaps at the beginning or end of your silent hour).

Listen to music—but really. Too often, we treat music as background noise. We play it while giving our primary attention to something else. Sit down with a favorite album, put away other distractions, and really and truly listen to it. Better yet, listen to live music. Best of all, *make* music with friends: Have a good old-fashioned hymn-sing, or get everyone to bring an instrument for an evening-long jam session.

Spend time with art that's worth time. Whether it's a painting, a museum, a play, or a finely crafted film, contemplate a work of art that in some way expresses the good, the true, and the beautiful. Ask: Does this make me wonder? As with what we just said about music, don't multitask. Afterward, take time to ruminate and discuss it with others.

COMMUNE. Spend an hour in the company of a good friend. You might do any of the above ideas together—the point is to also attend to each other. Forgo any agenda other than real, meaningful conversation. Make it a feast: Talk over tea and biscuits, or a well-brewed cup of coffee, a glass of wine, or a pint and a pipe; a little goes a long way in transforming an ordinary meeting into what Robert Farrar Capon calls a *session*.

When you've made time for good conversation, ask questions such as:

What's a book or article you've recently read that sheds new light on something?

What are you looking forward to in the next season?

What good gifts have you recently noticed? For what do you say "thank you"?

Who is someone you deeply admire and why?

How might I pray for you in the coming month?

Since it's the Sabbath, you might find your session stretching well past an hour, and blessedly, you'll be able to embrace it. Part of the goodness of living by a common rule is that you're all in it together. Receive this "waste of time" as a gift, a little foretaste of that eternal session, when we'll have all the time in the world.

Silence, aesthetic delight, communion. You and your community will come up with your own list of ideas. The key is that rest isn't instrumental. Rest isn't a means to another end (like greater productivity); it *is* the end. It isn't a "break" from our vocation, a pause in between the meaningful stuff, but belongs to our vocation. It prefigures the Sabbath rest we will be invited into. When we rest, we practice for eternity.

SAYING NO: TIME AND MONEY

The negation that Sabbath calls for is obvious: ceasing. But breaking from the cycle of endless productivity is easier said than done. The temptation to find our identity in what we produce and consume is as old as humanity. The people of ancient Israel worried that they'd hunger if they didn't collect manna on the Sabbath. They wanted a backup plan in case the Lord didn't deliver.

Our anxieties tell us a lot about what we fear, and what we believe (or don't believe) about God's love and care. Do we trust that God will sustain the world, and our lives, if we ceased working for a day? Do we believe we would still be valued if we were less productive?

This side of eternity we'll always struggle to fully believe these truths. That's why we need practices that help us relinquish control of the two things that seem most scarce: time and money.

First, we give up control of our time by ceasing from work. We tend to think of our time as just that—our own. We navigate stressful seasons by trying to exert greater control over our time, finding new windows of productivity and new tricks for maximizing results.

Sabbath calls us to relinquish this illusory sense of control.

My friend Emily went on to nursing school after she finished Brazos Fellows. She decided to keep going with her Sabbath practice, even though she was starting a highly competitive program, and to invite others into it, even though her colleagues were mostly secular. So she invited classmates over on Sunday afternoons for a potluck and games—even when Monday morning exams loomed. Lots of questions ensued: How are you not studying? Aren't you anxious? How can you possibly relax and take a whole day off?

In turns out, sharing a pot of soup around a table is a powerful witness. By inviting colleagues into a simple feast, Emily testified to the grace of God. She welcomed others to share in a common good: the truth that our time is not our own, and our life does not depend on our endless productivity. (Unsurprisingly, her studies did not suffer because she kept Sabbath. She finished the program successfully and got a great job.)

Second, we give up control of our money by giving. American Christians are on the whole stingy. On average, the American Christian gives 2.5 percent of their income to charity. Only one out of five Christians follows the tithing standard of giving at least 10 percent of their income to their local church.[8] How would it transform the church if that rate doubled? How would it expand our ability to feed the hungry, to care for members in crisis, to support the well-being of our clergy, to invest in beautiful music, art, and architecture—if only *half* of us gave a tenth to the Lord?

Or, to put it more precisely, gave *back* to the Lord. Everything already belongs to God, such that we technically don't "own" anything but only steward it. As we recite after the offering in my church, "All things come from you, and of your own have we given you" (1 Chron. 29:14 ESV).

To tithe, and to cease from work, is to reject the false gods of Time (*chronos*) and Mammon (wealth), worldly powers that demand our total allegiance. We trust our generous God who clothes the flowers of the field and provides food for the sparrows. We relinquish control, unclench our fists, and open up our hands. And we receive the gift that awaits us in the end: rest with God.

GETTING STARTED WITH SABBATH

How do you jump into practicing Sabbath? How do you begin this part of your common rule? My main advice is just to go for it! Don't be half-hearted. Dive in, committing together to cease, rest, embrace, and feast. Here are a few tips for beginning:

First, find a tangible way to mark Sabbath off from the rest of your week. Open your Sabbath by lighting a candle, asking God to make you receptive and to bless the coming of a day of rest (the opening collect of this chapter works well). Close your Sabbath with prayers of gratitude.

Second, keep handy a to-remember notebook. Inevitably, during your Sabbath day you'll think of all sorts of things you need to do come Monday. Rather than caving in or feeling stressed that you'll forget, keep a small notebook to jot down things you'll return to after Sabbath. That helps you mentally move on.

Third, embrace spontaneity. Resist the urge to over-schedule your Sabbath, to maximize embracing and feasting. Go to church, and see what comes your way in the rest of the day. Be receptive to whoever crosses your path, and unrushed in your time with others.

Fourth, keep it simple. Sometimes, the best feast is the easy, simple dinner. For a few summers, we've enjoyed Hot Dog Sundays, inviting anyone we talk to at church to bring over a side or beverage to share while we grill up a bunch of hot dogs. Our friends Mary and Cody do something similar: Snack Night. Everyone brings whatever they find in their pantry or fridge, and kids and adults alike snack from a heavily laden common table. Simple can be good.

Finally, two or three months in, reevaluate. Ask together, what's going well? What do we want to adjust? What high hopes do we need to let go of? What tendencies of productivity, or poor forms of "rest," have we slipped into? Have grace for yourself, and each other. Learning to receive the gift takes time—probably all the time you have.

If I could go back and talk to my ten-year-old self, who felt a bit guilty for enjoying ice cream on a Sunday, I'd say, "Don't! Receive the gift." Nobody *earns* Sunday afternoon ice cream, and sometimes we're given good things we don't deserve. A sweet treat enjoyed with your family is a foretaste of those eternal delights that await us.

But I'd also have some sympathy for my older church friend who's more dogmatic about "Sabbath," whom it would be too easy to sneer at as a prude. In a world enthralled with consumption, a world that tells us to never deny our desires, we could use a dose of abstinence. Maybe that doesn't mean renouncing ice cream shops. But if old-fashioned Sabbatarianism easily fell into joyless legalism, we've surely overcorrected in treating Sunday like just any other day.

The fullness of Sabbath means these are not competing values. Prayer and delight, ceasing and embracing, set-apart-from and deeply-attentive-to the world—these go hand in hand. "Steadfast love and faithfulness meet; righteousness and peace kiss each other" (Ps. 85:10 ESV).

As We Close

Eat dinner. Pray daily. Study theology. Keep Sabbath. These four practices comprise a common rule—they're things worth doing, and even more worth doing together.

When I graduated college, I didn't know what to do with my life, or even what the next step was. Looking back, I wish I'd been able to do something like Brazos Fellows—to live by a common rule with others. I'm sure that these practices of community, prayer, study, and Sabbath would have been immensely helpful as I figured out what life should look like.

It still might have taken me just as long to figure out my occupational path, though. The practices that comprise this common rule aren't tools—they aren't means to the end of discerning one's vocation as much as they *are* the vocation. They aren't ways of figuring out what the good life is; they are the good life.

I had the chance to discuss a draft of this book with a group of thoughtful undergraduate students. One said something that struck me: "I would hope that my life could look like this. But I just don't know if it will, unless I live with people who want this too."

What a telling statement. Sometimes we can see the good, and know it as good, but feel like it's not really something we can aim for.

Maybe that's how you feel—maybe you're coming to the end of this book and feeling like it's an idealistic vision but ultimately not realizable. It's great, but it's probably not doable for me.

If you feel that way, my biggest advice is this: Try. Try one of these practices, with one or two others, for six months. See what fruit it bears.

And as you practice life together, may you hear and respond to the call of Christ. As you eat, pray, study, and keep Sabbath, may you learn to recognize God's voice, better attend to the world He made, and love and serve your neighbors.

Further Resources

Sample Common Rule

You and your community will want to craft your own common rule together, and dating and signing it will help validate your intent. To help you get started, here's the rule that Brazos Fellows commit to every year.

As a community, Brazos Society members engage in spiritual disciplines with the aim of growth in Christ, guided by our shared commitment to the following *Common Rule*:

1. CHURCH. Society members will faithfully attend and participate in Sunday worship, and they will seek opportunities to serve within the parish.

2. PRAYER. Society members will pray Morning Prayer together on weekday mornings, and they will pray Evening Prayer or Compline with roommates, families, friends, or on their own. (They will also participate in Spiritual Direction monthly as a means of bringing their whole life into conversation with God.)

3. SHARED MEALS. Society members will gather weekly for a common meal, extending hospitality and welcome to one another.

4. STUDY. Society members will prepare well and participate actively in both Sunday catechesis classes and the course of theological study.

5. SABBATH. Society members will cease from work on Sundays, and they will actively reduce their use of media technologies throughout the week, in order to receive the gifts of worship, restorative rest, hospitable embrace of others, and feasting.

6. COMMUNITY. Society members will practice charity, humility, and peace toward one another, and they will strive to resolve all conflicts (disputes, hurts, violations of boundaries, resentments) with others directly and in a godly manner.

Reading Lists

Throughout this book, I've suggested quite a few different things your community might study together. Here's a larger list organized by topical questions:

Why and how should you study? How do you pursue truth together?

The Vice of Curiosity: An Essay on Intellectual Appetite, Paul J. Griffiths

Leisure: The Basis of Culture, Josef Pieper

Reading for the Love of God, Jessica Hooten Wilson

Called into Questions, Matthew Lee Anderson

What is the story of the church?

The First Thousand Years, Robert Louis Wilken

Turning Points: Decisive Moments in the History of Christianity, Mark A. Noll, David Komline, and Han-Luen Kantzer Komline

How did the early church understand and approach theology?

Heavenly Participation: The Weaving of a Sacramental Tapestry, Hans Boersma

The Spirit of Early Christian Thought, Robert Louis Wilken

How do we learn to pray?

On the Lord's Prayer: Tertullian, Cyprian & Origen

The Interior Castle, Teresa of Avila

(Consider also reading chapters 1–7 of Wilken's *The First Thousand Years* and chapters 1 and 2 of Wilken's *The Spirit of Early Christian Thought*)

How did the early church read Scripture?

Scripture as Real Presence: Sacramental Exegesis in the Early Church, Hans Boersma

Expositions on the Psalms (try the expositions of Psalm 1 and Psalm 37), Augustine

First Principles (try book IV, chapters 1–3), Origen

On Christian Doctrine, Augustine

(Consider also reading chapters 8–9 and 11–15 of Wilken's *The First Thousand Years* and chapter 3 of Wilken's *The Spirit of Early Christian Thought*)

How did the church come to understand Jesus Christ?

On the Incarnation, Athanasius

On God and Christ, The Five Theological Orations, Gregory of Nazianzus

On the Unity of Christ, Cyril of Alexandria

(Consider also reading chapters 17, 20, and 29 of Wilken's *The First Thousand Years* and chapters 4–6 of Wilken's *The Spirit of Early Christian Thought*)

What did early Christians believe about the body's role in the Christian life?

The Body and Society: Men, Women, and Sexual Renunciation, Peter Brown (try chapter 11)

The Sayings of the Desert Fathers

On Fasting and Feasts, Basil the Great

(Consider also reading chapter 10 of Wilken's *The First Thousand Years*)

How did the early church understand society?

Wealth and Poverty in Early Christianity, edited by Helen Rhee

On Social Justice, Basil the Great

The City of God (try book XIX), Augustine

(Consider also reading Stephen Presley, *Cultural Sanctification: Engaging the World Like the Early Church*; chapters 16, 18, and 21 of Wilken's *The First Thousand Years*; and chapters 7 and 8 of Wilken's *The Spirit of Early Christian Thought*)

What animated medieval Christian theology?

Summa Theologiae (try reading 1.2.3, 1.3.3–5, 1.4.2), Thomas Aquinas

The Divine Comedy (why not read along with the *100 Days of Dante* videos?), Dante

Revelations of Divine Love, Julian of Norwich

(Consider also reading chapters 3 and 4 of Boersma's *Heavenly Participation*)

What theology and practice emerged from the sixteenth-century Reformations?

Lutheran: *The Freedom of a Christian*, Martin Luther

Reformed: John Calvin's *Reply to Sadoleto* and John Bunyan's *Pilgrim's Progress*

English: Thomas Cranmer's introduction to the 1549 *Book of Common Prayer* and George Herbert's *The Complete Poetry*

Catholic: Francis de Sales, *Introduction to the Devout Life*

(Consider also reading chapter 5 of Boersma's *Heavenly Participation*)

How did evangelical revivals transform American Christianity?

On Revival (read "Distinguishing Marks"), Jonathan Edwards

Lectures on Revivals of Religion, Charles Finney

(Consider also reading Thomas Kidd's *The First Great Awakening* and Mark Noll's *The Civil War as a Theological Crisis*)

How did various Christian groups respond differently to modernity?

Liberal Protestantism: *On Religion* (First and Second Speeches), Frederick Schleiermacher

Fundamentalist-modernist debates: Harry Emerson Fosdick, "Shall the Fundamentalists Win?" and Clarence Macartney, "Shall Unbelief Win?"

Neo-orthodox Protestants: *Evangelical Theology: An Introduction* (chapters 1–9), Karl Barth

Vatican I Catholicism: "Syllabus of Errors" and Leo XIII's *Rerum Novarum*

Vatican II Catholicism: *Lumen Gentium*

Anglicans: *The Whimsical Christian*, Dorothy Sayers, and *The Abolition of Man*, C. S. Lewis

Others: *Foolishness to the Greeks: Gospel and Western Culture*, Lesslie Newbigin, and *After Virtue*, Alistair MacIntyre

How might we follow Christ's call today?

The Cost of Discipleship, Dietrich Bonhoeffer

Spe Salvi, Benedict XVI

For the Life of the World: Sacraments and Orthodoxy, Alexander Schmemann

Acknowledgments

This book owes much to good people and dear friends. I'm grateful to all who've shared community with Paige and me, especially the Kedesh house and the many members of Friday Night Dinner Group. The hours we've enjoyed around the table have been a great gift.

It's not possible to name all those who contribute to our community at Brazos Fellows: the people of Christ Church Waco, guest instructors, tutors, hosts, and those who partner with us in prayer and in giving. Special thanks to our board, Elizabeth and David Corey, Jeff and Debbie Wallace, Fr. Nicholas Norman-Krause, Matt Anderson, Alex Fogleman, and Hans Boersma, my colleagues Paige, Fr. Jonathan Kanary, Molly Fogleman, and Brooke Smith, and others who have given so much of themselves in caring for the fellows, especially Debbie Wallace and Alex Fogleman. What a joy to do this work with such excellent people.

It's been a privilege to pray, study, and share life with the Brazos Fellows. I'm grateful for each of them: to date, Jess, Emma, Sarah, Gene, Kelsey, Emily E., Emily V., Savannah Anne, Mitchell, Chris, Tiffany, Celeste, Belle, Brittany, Emma, Taylor, Rachel, Cara, Kathryn, Hannah, Emlee, Joel, Matt, Brooke, Brandi, Anndrea, Mitch, Daniel,

Alan, Milyna, Elizabeth, Jean, Jake, Claire, Liz, Griffin, and Hannah. "I thank my God in all my remembrance of you, always in every prayer of mine for you all making my prayer with joy, thankful for your partnership in the gospel from the first day until now" (Phil. 1:3–5).

Many have helped me in the process of this book. A special thank you to Matt Anderson for encouragement, introductions, and tacos—if you disliked the book, blame him for insisting that I write it. Thank you to Drew Dyck and Pam Pugh for believing in the project and helping it become the best possible version of itself. Thank you to those who shared stories or suggested voices I should bring in. Thank you to Josh Allen for an MVP season that inspired me while writing and revising. I received invaluable feedback from several reading groups: from Fr. Jonathan, Alex, Matt, Paige, and Cameron Doolittle, from Brazos Fellows alumni Mitchell Elequin, Celeste Widdows Gama, Joel Trigger, Jessica Schurz, and Elizabeth Hamilton, and from brilliant Baylor students: Melody Goh, Luke Pelser, Kiron Ang, Emma Freemyer, Madeline Peacock, and Jay Abbott. And thank you to Brittany McComb for the last-minute corrections. Any author would count themselves lucky to have readers so thoughtful and generous—thanks to each of you.

Speaking of generosity, in so many ways the Lord has given me "more than I either desire or deserve." Among these gifts is my family, including my parents, Jim and Sue Ellen, and my siblings, Esther, Hannah, Matt, and Lydia, whose love and support sustains me. I'm thankful for the prayers of my great-aunt Bernadine. I'm deeply grateful for the gift of our children James, Marianne, Matthew, and Joshua, who contribute to our community an endless supply of delight, laughter, children's books, Legos, and general noise. And finally, the gift of Paige: I love that we get to be a team not only in making a home and raising children but also in the fellowship. I'm so glad we get to practice life together.

Notes

The Trellis—An Introduction

1. J. I. Packer and Joel Scandrett, eds., *To Be a Christian: An Anglican Catechism* (Crossway, 2020), 17.
2. For great introductions to the spiritual disciplines, see two classics: Richard Foster, *Celebration of Discipline* (Harper & Row, 1976); and Dallas Willard, *The Spirit of the Disciplines: Understanding How God Changes Lives* (Harper & Row, 1988). A recent book that picks up Willard and presents many of his ideas afresh for today's readers is John Mark Comer's *Practicing the Way* (Random House, 2024).
3. The great church historian Robert Louis Wilken argues that from the fourth century through the Middle Ages "nothing was more vital to Christian life than monasticism. . . . It proved to be versatile, resilient, and adaptable." *The First Thousand Years* (Yale University Press, 2012), 108.

Chapter One—Breaking Bread: Life at the Table

1. Robert Louis Wilken, *The Spirit of Early Christian Thought* (Yale University Press, 2003), 40.
2. These thoughts are explored in Leon Kass's *The Hungry Soul: Eating and the Perfecting of Our Nature*.
3. Cyril, *Dialogue*, quoted in Jean-Marie R. Tillard, *Flesh of the Church, Flesh of Christ* (Liturgical Press, 2001), 76.

4. Chrysostom, *Homilies on First Corinthians*, quoted in Tillard, *Flesh of the Church*, 66–67.
5. Tillard, *Flesh of the Church*, 28.

Chapter Two—Life Together: The Gift and Challenge of Community

1. Hugh Feiss, "A Life of Listening," *Christian History* 93 (2007).
2. Dietrich Bonhoeffer, *Life Together* (Fortress Press, 2015), 75.
3. Bonhoeffer, *Life Together*, 75.
4. Henri J. M. Nouwen, *Bread for the Journey: A Daybook of Wisdom and Faith* (HarperCollins, 2006), March 11.
5. If you aren't yet convinced of the great cost we're paying through our smartphone addiction, read Jonathan Haidt's work, including *The Anxious Generation: How the Great Rewiring of Childhood Is Causing an Epidemic of Mental Illness* (Penguin, 2024).
6. Nouwen, *Bread for the Journey*, March 11.
7. See Luke 14:12–14; Matthew 25:42–46; Romans 12:13; Titus 1:8; 1 Timothy 3:2 and 5:10; 1 Peter 4:9.
8. "Mover's Remorse: Examining the Downstream Effects of Moving and Settling Down," Porch, https://porch.com/resource/movers-remorse.
9. Erica Pandey, "American the Single," Axios, February 25, 2023, https://www.axios.com/2023/02/25marriage-declining-single-dating-taxes-relationships.
10. Quoted in an excellent essay by Fr. Gerard D'Souza, "Monastic Stability: In One Place with God and Others," Front Porch Republic, https://www.frontporchrepublic.com/2015/10/monastic-stability-in-one-place-with-god-and-others/.
11. Rowan Williams, "The Staying Power of Benedict in Parliament Square," Charles Gore Lecture 2016, https://www.westminster-abbey.org/charles-gore-memorial-lectures/charles-gore-lecture-2016/.

Chapter Three—Practicing Weekly Dinner

1. Robert Farrar Capon, *Supper of the Lamb* (Modern Library, 2002), 27.
2. C. S. Lewis, *The Lion, the Witch and the Wardrobe* (HarperCollins, 1978), 82, 95.
3. Robert Louis Wilken, *The First Thousand Years* (Yale University Press, 2003), 105.
4. Basil of Caesarea, *On Fasting and Feasts* (St. Vladimir's Seminary Press, 2013), 112.

5. Dietrich Bonhoeffer, *Life Together* (Fortress Press, 2015), 48.
6. St. Basil, *On Fasting and Feasts*, 56.
7. Quoted in Lawrence J. Johnson, *Worship in the Early Church: An Anthology of Historical Sources* (Liturgical Press, 2009), 106.

Chapter Four—Speaking with God: The Life of Prayer

1. Alistair Stewart-Sykes, trans., annot., *On the Lord's Prayer: Tertullian, Cyprian & Origen* (St. Vladimir's Seminary Press, 2013), 42, 70.
2. Hans Urs von Balthasar, *Prayer* (Ignatius Press, 1986), 14.
3. Teresa of Avila, *The Interior Castle* (Paulist Press, 1979), 49.
4. Rowan Williams, *Being Christian: Baptism, Bible, Eucharist, Prayer* (Eerdmans, 2014), 62.
5. *On the Lord's Prayer: Tertullian, Cyprian & Origen* (St. Vladimir's Seminary Press), 66.
6. Comment made at "Tipsy Orthodoxy," a series of free theology talks hosted by Brazos Fellows at our local pub.
7. Teresa, *The Interior Castle*, 59.
8. *On the Lord's Prayer*, 79.
9. Teresa, *The Interior Castle*, 76.
10. *On the Lord's Prayer*, 63.
11. I'm grateful to Bruce Hindmarsh for sharing this story, drawn from Teresa's autobiography.
12. Rowan Williams, *Being Christian*, 65.
13. *On the Lord's Prayer*, 74.

Chapter Five—Keeping Time: Living in Rhythms of Prayer

1. *The Journals of Father Alexander Schmemann 1973–1983* (St. Vladimir's Seminary Press, 2013), 75.
2. "Learning to Tell Time Liturgically," The Living Church, November 20, 2015, https://covenant.livingchurch.org/2015/11/20/learning-to-tell-time-liturgically/.
3. Robert Louis Wilken, *The First Thousand Years* (Yale University Press, 2003), 37–39.
4. For a very helpful debunking of "the myth of 'pagan' Christmas," see an article by the same name written by historian Tom Holland and published at Unherd.com, December 25, 2021, https://unherd.com/2021/12/the-myth-of-pagan-christmas-2/.
5. See Wilken, *First Thousand Years*, 39.
6. If you're new to the church year, there are many great resources on

how to inhabit this drama:
- The InterVarsity series Fullness of Time features books written on each major liturgical season by leading theologians such as Esau McCaulley and Fleming Rutledge.
- The Let Us Keep the Feast book series offers insights and tips on observing the church calendar in your home or with your community.
- Anglican Compass publishes a free online "Rookie Anglican Guide to the Liturgical Year," with plenty of reading, prayers, and suggestions for how to embrace living out each season.
- Church calendars can be ordered from Ashby Publishing.

7. Quoted in Wilken, *The First Thousand Years*, 38.
8. *The Didache*, chapter 14.
9. Alexander Schmemann, *For the Life of the World* (St. Vladimir's Seminary Press, 2018), 39.
10. *The Didache*, chapter 8.
11. Quoted in Henry Chadwick, *The Early Church* (Penguin, 1993), 272. Chadwick adds, "Prayers at the third, sixth, and ninth hours are similarly mentioned by Tertullian, Cyprian, Clement of Alexandria and Origen, and must have been very widely practised. These prayers were commonly associated with private Bible reading in the family."
12. Jonathan Edwards wrote a book on self-examination, excerpts of which can be read here: http://digitalpuritan.net/jeonself-examination.
13. See John Wesley's twenty-two questions for self-examination, found here: https://www.umc.org/en/content/john-wesleys-22-questions-of-self-examination.
14. Richard Foster, *Celebration of Discipline* (Harper & Row, 1976).
15. This version comes from my friend Debbie, who adapted it from Fr. Joseph Tetlow's *Finding Christ in the World: A Twelve Week Ignatian Retreat in Everyday Life* (Institute of Jesuit Sources, 2017).
16. Annie Dillard, *The Writing Life* (Harper & Row, 1989), 32.

Chapter Six—Practicing Common Prayer

1. Thanks to Fr. Nicholas Norman-Krause for bringing my attention to this quote. Stanley Hauerwas, *Performing the Faith: Bonhoeffer and the Practice of Nonviolence* (Wipf & Stock, 2015), 22.
2. Alan Jacobs, *The Book of Common Prayer: A Biography* (Princeton University Press, 2013), 33.

3. For more great thoughts from Jess on the value of loneliness, see her post "Learning to Be Lonely" at the Brazos Fellows blog: https://brazosfellowsblog.wordpress.com/2018/12/03/learning-to-be-lonely/.
4. Dietrich Bonhoeffer, *Life Together: Prayerbook of the Bible* (Fortress Press, 2015), 57.
5. Much of what follows in this section is adapted from the Brazos Societies Handbook, which can be requested at brazossocieties.com.
6. For more practical guidance on beginning, check out the resources put together by AnglicanCompass.com, titled "Getting Started with the Daily Office: A Rookie Anglican Guide."

Chapter Seven—Loving the Lord with All Our Mind: The Life of Study

1. For the fascinating life of Timothy I, see Robert Louis Wilken, *The First Thousand Years* (Yale University Press, 2012), 308–15.
2. Paul J. Griffiths, *The Vice of Curiosity: An Essay on Intellectual Appetite* (Wipf & Stock, 2018), 60.
3. Griffiths, *The Vice of Curiosity*, 61.
4. Thanks to Hans Boersma for this quotation from Augustine's *Confessions* 10.35.55.
5. Griffiths, *The Vice of Curiosity*, 16.
6. See the American Time Use Survey results here: Bureau of Labor Statistics, US Department of Labor, *Economics Daily*, "Time Spent Reading for Personal Interest in 2020," https://www.bls.gov/opub/ted/2021/time-spent-reading-for-personal-interest-in-2020.htm; Rachel Krantz-Kent, "Television, Capturing America's Attention at Prime Time and Beyond," *Beyond the Numbers* 7, no. 14 (September 2018), https://www.bls.gov/opub/btn/volume-7/television-capturing-americas-attention.htm.
7. Jeffrey Jones, "Americans Reading Fewer Books than in Past," *Gallup*, https://news.gallup.com/poll/388541/americans-reading-fewer-books-past.aspx#.
8. For a wonderful defense of ordinary intellectual life, see Zena Hitz's book *Lost in Thought: The Hidden Pleasures of an Intellectual Life* (Princeton University Press, 2020).
9. Griffiths, *The Vice of Curiosity*, 77.
10. Augustine, *Confessions*, I.20.31.
11. From a 1542 letter, quoted by Fr. Brian J. Lehane: http://bradt56.blogspot.com/2015/06/attitude-of-gratitude-examen-prayer-of.html.
12. Robert Farrar Capon, *The Supper of the Lamb* (Random House, 2002), 17.

13. Capon, *The Supper of the Lamb*, 19.
14. Gilbert K. Chesterton, *Orthodoxy* (John Lane, 1909), 108–9.
15. For an excellent account of the role of questions in the Christian life, see Matthew Lee Anderson's *Called into Questions* (Moody, 2023).
16. This commencement speech is available online: https://leadingwithquestions.com/teaching/a-few-questions-for-you/.
17. *The Prayers and Meditations of Saint Anselm with the Proslogion*, trans. Sr. Benedicta Ward (Penguin Books, 1973), 239–40.

Chapter Eight—Our Inheritance: Receiving the Gift of Tradition

1. Immanuel Kant, "What Is Enlightenment," trans. Peter Gay in *The Enlightenment: A Comprehensive Anthology* (Simon & Schuster, 1973), 384.
2. Peter De Vries, *The Tents of Wickedness* (Little, Brown and Co., 1959), 6.
3. Jaroslav Pelikan, interview with *US News & World Report*, July 26, 1989, quoted in *Harper's Magazine*, https://harpers.org/2008/12/pelikan-on-tradition-and-traditionalism/.
4. Yves Congar, *The Meaning of Tradition* (Ignatius Press, 2004), 3.
5. C. S. Lewis, *Surprised by Joy* (Harcourt, Brace, Jovanovich, 1966), 207.
6. C. S. Lewis, introduction to *Athanasius: The Incarnation of the Word of God*, trans. a Religious of C.S.M.V. (Macmillian, 1946), 7.
7. Lewis, introduction to *Athanasius*, 7.

Chapter Nine—Practicing Reading Together

1. See chapter 2 in Alan Jacobs, *How to Think: A Survival Guide for a World at Odds* (Crown Currency, 2017).
2. Jacobs, *How to Think*, 63.
3. Craig Allert, *A High View of Scripture* (Baker, 2007), 173.
4. Augustine, *Exposition on the Psalms*, https://www.newadvent.org/fathers/1801.htm.
5. Hilary of Poitiers, *Homilies on the Psalms*, https://www.newadvent.org/fathers/3303.htm.
6. Bernard of Clairvaux, *Monastic Sermons*, trans. Daniel Griggs (Cistercian, 2016).
7. For example, see the exhibition on Psalm 147: https://thevcs.org/song-thanksgiving/alleluia-first-and-last.
8. Popular Patristics Series, SVS Press, https://svspress.com/categories/Popular-Patristics-Series/.

Notes

9. See here: https://holyjoys.org/church-fathers-reading-list/.
10. Alan Jacobs, *Breaking Bread with the Dead: A Reader's Guide to a More Tranquil Mind* (Penguin, 2020), 29.
11. For a great example of this kind of reading, see Jessica Hooten Wilson's *Reading for the Love of God* (Brazos Press, 2023).
12. For great ideas on how to craft an opening question, read this by Fred Sanders: https://www.patheos.com/blogs/scriptorium/2013/07/the-opening-question-torrey-101/.
13. For a summary and response to Matt's call to quit Netflix, see Brett McCracken, "Should You Quit Netflix?," Gospel Coalition, June 29, 2019, https://www.thegospelcoalition.org/article/quit-netflix/.
14. My thinking on this—and my classroom policies—have been shaped by Alan Jacobs's. See https://ayjay.org/FAQ.html.
15. Brandon Keim, "Why the Smart Reading Device of the Future May Be . . . Paper," Wired, May 1, 2014, https://www.wired.com/2014/05/reading-on-screen-versus-paper/.

Chapter Ten—Preparing to Die: Living Our Vocation

1. My friend Fr. Jonathan Kanary points out that anchorites were required to have adequate financial support, and extant wills show people leaving anchorites such support. In other words, they didn't languish or beg—they were taken care of.
2. W. H. Auden, *The Shield of Achilles* (Random House, 1955), 67–68.
3. Auden, *The Shield of Achilles*, 74–75.
4. Quoted in Wilken, *The Spirit of Early Christian Thought*, 120–21.
5. Dietrich Bonhoeffer, *The Cost of Discipleship* (Simon & Schuster, 1995), 89.
6. C. S. Lewis, *Mere Christianity* (Touchstone, 1996), 190–91.
7. Quoted in Peter Kreeft, *Catholic Christianity* (Ignatius Press, 2001), 89.

Chapter Eleven—Hearing His Voice: The Lifelong Project of Discernment

1. Greg Iacurci, "2022 Was the 'Real Year of the Great Resignation,' Says Economist," CNBC, February 1 2023, https://www.cnbc.com/2023/02/01/why-2022-was-the-real-year-of-the-great-resignation.html.
2. Editorial Team, "17 Remarkable Career Change Statistics to Know," ApolloTechnical, September 17, 2024, https://www.apollotechnical.com/career-change-statistics/.

3. Ben adds: "At the very least we should recognize how connected our ability to discern and commit ourselves to our present responsibilities and roles is to our success in any future roles we might play." Benjamin Norquist, "Vocation," in *Life Questions Every Student Asks*, eds. Gary M. Burge and David Lauber (IVP Academic, 2020), 26.
4. Quoted by Paige Gutacker in a vocation seminar.
5. For one biblical scholar's interpretation of this period of Paul's life, see Ben Witherington's *Paul of Arabia: The Hidden Years of the Apostle to the Gentiles* (Wipf & Stock, 2020).
6. For more on Cassian's strategies, see Jamie Kreiner's *The Wandering Mind: What Medieval Monks Tell Us About Distraction* (Liveright, 2024).
7. If you'd like an introduction to the practice of *lectio*, I highly recommend a recent book by Hans Boersma, *Pierced by Love: Divine Reading with the Christian Tradition* (Lexham Press, 2023).

Chapter Twelve—Practicing Sabbath
1. Augustine, *The City of God*, book 22, chapter 30.
2. Alexander Schmemann, *For the Life of the World: Sacraments and Orthodoxy* (St. Vladimir's Seminary Press, 2018), 26.
3. Schmemann, *For the Life of the World*, 27.
4. Josef Pieper, *Leisure: The Basis of Culture* (Ignatius Press, 2018), 46–47.
5. Gordon Smith, *Listening to God in Times of Choice: The Art of Discerning God's Will* (InterVarsity Press, 2009), 70.
6. Pieper, *Leisure*, 46.
7. Gerard Manley Hopkins, "Pied Beauty."
8. "What Is a Tithe? New Data on the Perceptions of the 10 Percent," Barna Group, September 7, 2022, https://www.barna.com/research/what-is-a-tithe/.